These Words

These Words

Poetic Midrash on the Language of Torah

ALDEN SOLOVY

Foreword by Rabba Yaffa Epstein

CCAR
Press

CENTRAL CONFERENCE OF AMERICAN RABBIS

5783 New York 2023

*For the faculty, staff, and administration of the
Pardes Institute of Jewish Studies,
where I learned how to learn Torah. —Alden Solovy*

Copyright © 2023 by the Central Conference of American Rabbis

Published by Reform Judaism Publishing, a division of CCAR Press
355 Lexington Avenue, New York, NY 10017
(212) 972-3636 | info@ccarpress.org | www.ccarpress.org

LIBRARY OF CONGRESS CATALOGING-IN-PUBLICATION DATA
Names: Solovy, Alden T., 1957- author. | Epstein, Yaffa (Rabba), writer of
  preface.
Title: These words: poetic midrash on the language of Torah / Alden Solovy; foreword by
Rabba Yaffa Epstein.
Description: New York: Central Conference of American Rabbis, 2023. |
  Includes index. | Summary: "Echoing the midrash that the Torah has
  seventy faces, Solovy selects seventy of its Hebrew words. For each
  word, he delves into its etymology, translation, and usage, providing
  deeper insights into familiar texts. Then Solovy presents a poem-"poetic
  midrash"-inspired by and interpreting each word"-- Provided by
  publisher.
Identifiers: LCCN 2022050746 (print) | LCCN 2022050747 (ebook) | ISBN
  9780881236156 (trade paperback) | ISBN 9780881236163 (ebook)
Subjects: LCSH: Bible. Old Testament--Criticism, interpretation, etc.,
  Jewish. | Hebrew language--Religious aspects--Judaism. | Jewish
  religious poetry. | Jewish religious poetry, American. | Bible--In
  literature.
Classification: LCC BS1186 .S65 2023 (print) | LCC BS1186 (ebook) | DDC
  221.6--dc23/eng/20221206
LC record available at https://lccn.loc.gov/2022050746
LC ebook record available at https://lccn.loc.gov/2022050747

Cover calligraphy by Peretz Wolf-Prusan

Design and composition by Scott-Martin Kosofsky
at The Philidor Company, Rhinebeck, NY

Printed in the United States of America
10 9 8 7 6 5 4 3 2 1 0

*Publication of this book has been made possible in part
by a generous bequest from the estate of
Rabbi Samuel Egal Karff, z"l (1931–2020).
Rabbi Karff, a man of deep faith, a lover of language
and a teller of stories, understood the power
of words to touch the soul.*

Contents

THE COVER of *These Words: Poetic Midrash on the Language of Torah* features calligraphy of the phrase *eilu d'varim* jumping boldly from a background of Torah text.

The phrase *eilu d'varim*, literally 'these are the things,' opens a set of passages in our siddur recited in the Torah study portion of our daily liturgy. In *Mishkan T'filah*, the paragraph combines language found in the Mishnah's *Masechet Pei-ah* and the Talmud's *Masechet Shabbat*, teaching us core Jewish values, from honoring our parents to making peace. At the end of that list, we learn that the study of Torah encompasses them all.

The word *d'varim*, as you'll read in this volume, means not only 'things' but also 'words.' On our cover, *eilu d'varim* becomes a word-play worthy of a book about language. By using this phrase, we also summon the idea that the study of Torah is a core value, in this book reflected as the study and interpretation of individual words of Torah.

The Torah text behind the calligraphy is from Exodus chapters 36 and 37, which is the building of the *Mishkan*, another word we'll explore. This text is also fitting for our cover, as the *Mishkan* represents the yearning for a direct and personal relationship with God that comes, at least in part, from studying Torah. With due respect for God's holy name, care has been given to fading beyond readability the several uses of the Tetragrammaton in these columns of Torah.

Cover design by Scott-Martin Kosofsky
Calligraphy by Rabbi Peretz Wolf-Prusan

Foreword

Rabba Yaffa Epstein

מַאי תּוֹרָה? מִדְרַשׁ תּוֹרָה!

What is Torah? Midrash is Torah.

—Babylonian Talmud, *Kiddushin* 49b

הִלֵּל אוֹמֵר, הֱוֵי מִתַּלְמִידָיו שֶׁל אַהֲרֹן, אוֹהֵב שָׁלוֹם וְרוֹדֵף שָׁלוֹם,
אוֹהֵב אֶת הַבְּרִיּוֹת וּמְקָרְבָן לַתּוֹרָה.

Hillel says: Be a disciple of Aaron, loving peace and pursuing peace,
loving people, and bringing them closer to the Torah.

—*Pirkei Avot* 1:12

THERE IS NO BETTER description of Alden Solovy than as a student of Aaron, who loves and pursues peace. And there is no better description of his work than as a tool to bring people closer to the Torah.

I got to know Alden when he was a student in my siddur class at the Pardes Institute of Jewish Studies in Jerusalem. He was already deeply involved in the writing of poetry and liturgy, and yet he displayed his characteristic humility in his desire to continue growing and learning. The Jerusalem Talmud (*B'rachot* 5:2) teaches, "If I do not have understanding, how can I pray?" Alden knew instinctively that delving into the history, development, and meaning of Jewish prayer would bring him into a depth of understanding that would allow him to create even more beautiful, heartfelt prayers.

In this work, Alden takes on a new challenge, that of poetic midrash. Alden has set himself on a mission to investigate seventy Hebrew words of Torah—each one representing a core idea of Jewish wisdom. His essays delve deeply into each word's etymological roots, as well as a vast array of interpretations in Rabbinic, medieval, Chasidic, and modern Torah scholarship. Each essay is unique; Alden allows the word itself to guide him. Then he humbly offers up his own interpretations, weaving together millennia of scholars who came before him to create an entirely new interpretation that resonates with the intellectual sensibilities and spiritual realities of our day. He breathes new life into these beautiful Hebrew words, these divine gifts of inspiration. This is the holy practice of midrash.

One of the most beloved and challenging tales in the Babylonian Talmud (*M'nachot* 29b) tells the story of Moses receiving the Torah at Sinai. When Moses ascends the mountain, he sees God tying crowns onto the letters of the Torah. Moses is curious and asks God why these crowns are necessary. God answers that in the future, a great man named Akiva ben Yosef would teach heaps and heaps of laws from every point of each crown. Moses asks to meet this great man who would expound and expand upon the Torah that he was receiving that very day. God concurs, sending Moses to Rabbi Akiva's *beit midrash* (house of study). When he arrives, Moses does not understand the conversation, and he is saddened and overwhelmed. Then, he hears a student ask Rabbi Akiva for the source of one of his midrashic interpretations. Rabbi Akiva responds that it is a *halachah l'Moshe mi-Sinai*, 'a law given to Moses at Sinai'—a received tradition not based on midrashic interpretation but handed down from generation to generation. Moses hears this and is comforted.

This story teaches us that Torah must not be confined to the simple letters on a page, nor to the simple understanding of the text. Rabbi Akiva understands that God has written into Torah an invitation to each generation to expand upon these divine words, claiming them as our own. At the same time, the Talmud adjures that while we can—and must—add our own voices and perspectives, we must understand ourselves to always be a part of the glorious tradition that we have inherited. This is the work of the midrashist, to stay faithful to the past while also innovating.

Rabbi Jonathan Sacks, *z"l*, explains midrash in just this way: "Midrash is the attempt on the part of the sages to understand their own times as a continuation of the narrative of the covenant" (*The Chief Rabbi's Haggadah*, 95).

While at times it may feel that the depth and weight of Jewish tradition can restrict our words and our creativity, Alden shows, with this beautiful work, that delving into previous interpretations of generations of scholars, thinkers, and seekers only expands our potential to unlock new meaning for our generation. The old feeds the new rather than suffocating it.

Medieval *parshanim* (commentators) dance with Modern Hebrew scholars, historians are in dialogue with mystics, and etymologists encounter the Rabbis of the Talmud. The unifying thread is their ability to uncover the mysteries of Torah, as we discover myriad pathways to the Divine. *These Words* continues in the expansive tradition of Rabbi Akiva. Alden too has interpreted the crowns of each letter and opened the doors of Torah study to all who wish to enter. Gate after gate of meaning is unlocked, taking us into the depths that each word of Torah contains.

He then asks us to take these words and give them our own meaning, adding our own voices and breath to the sounds, coaxing our souls through the words of his midrashim, themselves both poems and prayers. It is no accident that Alden's final midrash is called "Ours Now," where he calls on us to search our lives, hearts, and minds for God's voice and to send our own voices as "signs" back to the Divine. May we merit to live up to his charge.

RABBA YAFFA EPSTEIN is the senior scholar and educator in residence at the Jewish Education Project. Previously, she was the director of the Wexner Heritage Program at the Wexner Foundation. She also served as the director of education, North America, for the Pardes Institute of Jewish Studies and was a member of the faculty for over fifteen years. She received Orthodox rabbinic ordination from Yeshivat Maharat, earned an additional private Orthodox ordination from Rabbi Daniel Landes, holds a law degree from Bar-Ilan University, and studied at the Talmud Department at Hebrew University. She has trained rabbis and educators from across the spectrum of Jewish denominations and is passionate about making Torah and Jewish learning accessible, exciting, and inclusive for all who wish to participate.

Acknowledgments

אֵלֶּה מַסְעֵי בְנֵי־יִשְׂרָאֵל אֲשֶׁר יָצְאוּ מֵאֶרֶץ מִצְרַיִם
לְצִבְאֹתָם בְּיַד־מֹשֶׁה וְאַהֲרֹן:

These were the marches of the Israelites who started out from the
land of Egypt, troop by troop, in the charge of Moses and Aaron.

—Numbers 33:1

IN NUMBERS 33, the Torah presents a systematic review of the
Israelites' journey from Egypt to Israel. Of the chapter's fifty-six
verses, forty-two begin with the word *vayisu*, alternatively translated as
'they set out,' 'they departed,' and 'they journeyed.' The root of *vayisu* is
nun-samech-ayin, meaning 'to pull out, to set out, to depart, to journey.'
The word appears in the Modern Hebrew parting expression for travel-
ers, *n'siah tovah*, 'a good journey.'

Creating this book has been a good journey, and many of you—my
rabbis, teachers, and friends—helped along the way. First, always first,
thank you to my readers. You have supported my writing for more
than a decade. You have encouraged the exploration of my poetic and
liturgical voices, and you have challenged me to push my creative lim-
its. Thank you for reading, sharing, and commenting on my work
online, for acquiring my books, and for using my writing in personal
and communal prayer, sometimes in the most intimate and challenging
moments of your lives. Thank you to those of you who have come to
synagogues, gatherings, and virtual events to hear me speak, as well as
those who have participated in my online teaching. You have made art
from my writing, created songs from my words, and have—literally—
choreographed my words into dance. You've embroidered my words
onto tallitot, have engraved them onto headstones, and have chanted
them with haftarah trope.

Thanks to the clergy, educators, synagogue directors, organizational
leaders, and the leaders of online Jewish platforms who've given me
opportunities to write and to teach throughout North America, in the

United Kingdom, and in Israel. I am particularly grateful for the partnerships that have evolved over the years, both with individual clergy and with your congregations.

Like the Israelites on the trip from Egypt to Israel, a host of people came along on this journey. Throughout the process of writing *These Words: Poetic Midrash on the Language of Torah*, I engaged with friends—in person and online—exploring words of Torah. Local friends lent me books and spent time talking Torah. I posted more than thirty questions on Facebook looking for a variety of resources—including books, references, source texts, explanations, and translations—yielding hundreds of responses. Several of you responded multiple times, including sending photos of pages of books to which I did not have access.

These people provided materials or answered Facebook posts that directly impacted my research or my approach: Rabbi Jake Best Adler, Gil Elon Amminadav, Rabbi Michael Bernstein, Amanda Borschel-Dan, Sara Brandes, Debbie Brookfield, Warren Burstein, Rabbi Don Cashman, Arnie Draiman, Dvir Falik, Ilana Foss, Everett Fox, Rabbi Gordon Fuller, Deborah Greniman, Ruz Gulko, Rabbi Joel M. Hoffman, Jonathan Howard, Rabbi Aytan Kadden, Shifra Kadden, Nadia Kahan, David Kaplinsky, Rabbi Rick Kellner, Rabbi Riqi Kosovske, Cecile Kowalski, Rabbi Lily Kowalski, Halima Krausen, Rabbah Nathalie Lastreger, Eryn London, Rabbi Ari Lorge, Jacquie Marx, Simon Montagu, Rabbi Lea Mühlstein, Aneesha Parrone, Ericka Riddick, Cantor Alyssa Rosenbaum, Rachel Roth, Suzanne Sabransky, Rabbi Jeff Salkin, Barbara Seaver, Tamar Neuhaus Selch, Hilary Silver, Rabbi Daniel Raphael Silverstein, Rabbi Jennifer Singer, Rabbi Jonathan Slater, Michael Slater, Sandy Starkman, Jordyn (Yarden) Steifman, Rebecca Sykes, Ma'ayan Turner, Haim Watzman, and Dina Weiner. My apologies to anyone I missed. I spent hours with my friend, running partner, hiking buddy, and Talmud *chavruta* Asher Arbit talking about words of Torah. He lent me books and insights.

Thanks to the creators and contributors of two online resources that were critical to my research: Sefaria.org and Alhatorah.org. Each day that I conducted research for this book, multiple windows of each of these tools were open on my desktop. My gratitude also goes to the authors of three online Torah and Hebrew-language resources: David Curwin, author of *Balashon: Hebrew Language Detective*; Rabbi Reuven

Chaim Klein, author of *What's in a Word?*; and Dr. Jeremy Benstein, author of *The Hebrew Corner* on the 929-English website.

Learning Torah is a skill, an art, and a passion and is central to the creation of *These Words*. Every teacher whom I have encountered has influenced my Jewish heart and soul, and thus my writing. I learned how to learn Torah at the Pardes Institute of Jewish Studies, Jerusalem. Here I list the faculty there with whom I learned text study—a formidable list: Rabbanit Nechama Goldman Barash, Rav Rahel Berkovits, Rabbi Levi Cooper, Rav Mike Feuer, Gila Fine, Rabbi Michael Hattin, Rabbi Zvi Hirschfield, Judy Klitsner, Rabbi Dov Laimon, Tovah Leah Nachmani, Elisa Pearlman, Jamie Salter, Rabbi Meir Schweiger, and Yiscah Smith. My gratitude also goes to Rabbi Howard Markose, my Biblical Hebrew grammar teacher, whose passion for Hebrew is second to none. He served as an ongoing resource as I pursued understanding of the words in this volume. Two Pardes students provided research, each on one word of Torah: Joe Blumberg and Manny Samuels. I would also like to acknowledge two former faculty members who were my first teachers at Pardes and have encouraged my writing ever since: Rabba Yaffa Epstein and Rabbi David Levin-Kruss. I am also grateful to the entire dedicated staff of Pardes, who have supported and encouraged my learning. Special thanks to my teachers, dean emeritus Dr. David I. Bernstein and the president, Rabbi Leon A. Morris, for inviting me to serve as the institution's liturgist in residence, opening doors for my learning and teaching.

A story: early in my *aliyah* to Jerusalem, a new friend by the name of Fern Reiss invited me to her home for Shabbat dinner. At the time, I didn't know how important that Friday night meal would become. Fern, an author's consultant, became my advisor for self-publishing my first two volumes, launching me into the world of publishing. I still have great gratitude for her wisdom and dedication. At her Shabbat table, I met Rabba Epstein, who brought me to Pardes where I became a devoted student of Yaffa and a friend. What a joy and an honor to share the cover of this book with Yaffa, who wrote a beautiful foreword to the volume. Thank you, my friend, for your kind and inspiring words. I am deeply moved.

This book is profoundly influenced by another friend, Avital Ordan. A research librarian with a passion for Hebrew, she responded to numerous online queries. Avital used her access to the library at The Hebrew University to find books that I needed, check references, and find and confirm translations, at times connecting me to others who might have a needed insight or reference. As a result of her enthusiasm, knowledge, and skills, she served as technical reviewer for this volume, offering insights and suggestions on almost every *d'var Torah*, as well as several of the poems. A special thanks to her, as well.

Thank you to Rabbi Barry H. Block, Rabbi Angela Warnick Buchdahl, and Dr. Everett Fox for your heartfelt and generous endorsements.

My writing is carried by the love and support of my family and friends. To my mother and sisters, thank you for your love and encouragement. To my daughters, Nikki and Dana, both writers, I cherish our conversations about writing, writers, and books. Your support and enthusiasm for my work mean more to me than I can express here.

Thanks to the CCAR Press professional team who have supported this enterprise. Thank you, Deborah Smilow and Chiara Ricisak. Special thanks to Raquel Fairweather for your enthusiasm, professionalism, and ongoing efforts in marketing and promoting all our collaborations. Thanks to copyeditor Debra Hirsch Corman, who has applied her skills to each of my CCAR Press volumes, showing a deep understanding of my work and a commitment to its integrity. Thanks also to Michelle Kwitkin for proofreading and Scott-Martin Kosofsky for design, each of whom also worked their magic on my previous CCAR Press books. Along with internal design, Scott designed this volume's stunning cover, using the beautiful calligraphy of Rabbi Peretz Wolf-Prusan as the central feature.

I continue to be impressed by the vision of the CCAR Press team. The questions, insights, and editorial skills of press director Rafael Chaiken and editor Rabbi Jan Katz were critical to the quality of this volume. A special thanks to Rafael for dedicating the time of two rabbinic interns to this project. Both Ada Luisa Sinacore and Ariel Tovlev provided research on several of the words included in the book. Their support was invaluable.

This journey—from idea to book—began as did my other three CCAR Press books: over coffee in Jerusalem with Rabbi Hara Person, the organization's chief executive. Although I am not a rabbi, Hara—my mentor and friend—has made me part of the CCAR family. Thanks to the CCAR Press Council for supporting this project. I am honored that Rabbi Donald Goor, chair of the committee, continues to advocate for my work, as he has since the beginning of my relationship with CCAR.

It seems to me that writing the acknowledgments for a book is one of the most perilous parts of the journey. I wonder who I might forget, perhaps someone who was a guiding star whom I have inadvertently left out. If that is you, please accept my apology.

With deep love, once more, for you my reader—and with gratitude to the Holy One of Blessing for the gift of Torah and the desire to explore it—may *These Words* enliven and enlighten our lives.

Introduction

תּוֹרָה צִוָּה לָנוּ מֹשֶׁה מוֹרָשָׁה קְהִלַּת יַעֲקֹב.
Moses charged us with the Teaching,
as the heritage of the congregation of Jacob.
—Deuteronomy 33:4

WHEN I WAS IN ELEMENTARY SCHOOL, I was told that I'd never be able to learn to read Hebrew. My brain played tricks on Hebrew letters. I'd never be able to distinguish between the letters *hei* and *chet* or between a *mem*, a *samech*, and a final *mem*. And forget about the vowels— my brain would make a *segol* into a *kamatz* and a *tzeireh* into a *patach*. The idea that I would never learn to read Hebrew was a gut punch. It felt as if the full heritage of Torah could never be completely mine.

It was the 1960s, not long after the term "learning disability" was coined. I was tested; I was told my limitations. It felt like the harsh judgments of the elders. The story I tell myself is that my teachers were doing the best they could with the tools they had at the time. I tell myself that there are now so many more teaching tools available, no educator would slam the door shut like that on a child's learning. True or not, these stories allow me to forgive.

We are a people of stories. We tell them. Then we tell stories about them. Then we tell stories about the stories of the stories. We call that midrash. This tradition of expanding Torah invites us to explore. It also allows us to hold multiple truths, like acknowledging the simple truth that my grade-school teachers hurt me emotionally and harmed my education, while at the same time exploring the story that they were doing their best. They were wrong. To this day I make all the mistakes predicted by my teachers. Reading Hebrew takes serious concentration and effort. Some days are easier than others. Just ask my *chavruta*, who puts up with the variability of my reading efforts. I have become a perfectly imperfect student of the Hebrew language.

Hebrew words have weight, spiritual heft, emotional magnetism, mystical illuminations. There are secrets waiting to be found in them:

in the vowels, the letters, the words, the grammatical structures, the uses, the etymologies, and the mythologies. We tell stories about our words, stories that have become part of the ethos of the Jewish people.

These Words: Poetic Midrash on the Language of Torah is a book of stories about words of Torah, a book about their history, how they are used, and what they mean. Based on the stories that have been told about these words for generations, this book offers new stories—my own poetic midrashim on words from the Torah.

Midrash and Poetic Midrash

Jacob Neusner defines 'midrash' as "biblical exegesis by ancient Judaic authorities using a mode of interpretation prominent in the Talmud." It is used in three ways, to mean biblical interpretation, a method of interpretation, or a collection of those interpretations. More recently, My Jewish Learning states, midrash has been used to include an "interpretive act, seeking the answers to religious questions (both practical and theological) by plumbing the meaning of the words of the Torah." The definition has come to include the visual and performing arts.

In 1999, the Institute for Contemporary Midrash held "The Future of Midrash: A Scholars and Artists Convocation." Between 1997 and 2000, that organization published eight semiannual volumes of contemporary midrash, including a wide variety of poetry. Variations of the term 'poetic midrash' have appeared on websites as diverse as the Jewish Pluralist and the Times of Israel.

Women have led the creation of poetic midrash. In the Jewish Women's Archive, poet and educator Jessica Rosenfeld notes, "A growing trend, one that is rooted in the English and Yiddish poetry of the late nineteenth and early twentieth centuries, is for Jewish women poets to add their voices to the sacred texts of Judaism through poetry." Rosenfeld identifies poet Alicia Ostriker as "one of the more playful experimenters with poetic midrash." Ostriker writes, "Traditional midrash may be homiletic, witty, mystical, wildly imaginative; it is always, however, deeply religious in intent. Contemporary midrash, as the term has been widely and loosely used for several decades, may take the form of poetry, fiction, drama and bibliodrama based on biblical narratives, as well as visual art, film, and music. Like traditional midrash, contemporary midrash addresses itself to the potential meanings of scripture in one's present moment, and to pressing psychological and social issues in one's present community."

Poetry has moved into the mainstream of midrashic exploration, providing a powerful vehicle both for a gentle rethinking of ancient tales and for a radical reenvisioning of the content and the intent of what we find in the Torah. It gives us a new doorway into questions that haven't yet been asked and a technique for asking questions that cannot be answered. Poetic device has become a new currency of interpretation and understanding, both for breaking with tradition and reinforcing it. This volume gives individual words found in the Torah a bold, powerful, introspective, lyrical, and poetic voice.

Selection and Organization

In the midrash (*B'midbar Rabbah* 13:16), the Sages say that there are *shivim panim laTorah*, 'seventy faces of Torah.' This teaches that there are myriad ways to interpret Torah, and it is for us to explore them. Together with the publisher, I've selected seventy words to examine in this book, representing the midrashic idea that there is always more Torah left to be discovered. Ben Bag-Bag declares, "Turn it, and turn it over again, for everything is in it. Reflect on it and grow old and gray with it. Don't turn from it, for nothing is better than it" (*Pirkei Avot* 5:25).

Readers of *These Words* may wonder: from the thousands of distinct words of Torah, how was this list of seventy created? I began by selecting my own words of interest and then put a question on Facebook asking friends to share words of Torah that they love, that challenge them, or that they want to learn more about. The combined list included more than 250 words. In the process of culling that list down to an initial seventy, other words came to mind. This was a recurring theme throughout the writing: one word hinting at the need to look at another. Of the final seventy, twelve were not on the original list. In all, I looked at more than 130 words. The process was more art than science.

Grouping the words into chapters was also more art than science, in large part because the words were selected individually without chapter groupings in mind. As a result, several of the words could be equally well categorized into several of the chapters. The first half of the book follows the story of Torah writ large: God, Creation, humanity, journeys, and peoplehood. The second half addresses our relationships with God and each other, categorized as mitzvot, offerings, holy time, mysteries, and love.

Each word is presented here on its own two-page spread. On the left-hand page is a brief narrative discussion of each word—a *d'var Torah* on each of the entries. These discussions are neither exhaustive nor definitive. Indeed, I have many more notes on each word than I could use, running to hundreds of pages in total. Rather, the left-hand pages focus primarily on the information that informs the poetic midrash. The right-hand page contains the resulting poetry.

In writing this book, I have attempted to honor two distinct but intertwining projects: the scholarly project of understanding word origins, and the Rabbinic project of unpacking and at times creating spiritual understanding from them. It should be noted that what a rabbi declares as a word's root doesn't always match the scholarly research. Moreover, linguistic scholars regularly disagree on etymologies. I've endeavored to create space for each of these voices, sometimes blending them, sometimes contrasting them.

Although the result of serious research, this book is a poetic rather than scholarly work. It contains two varieties of poetic midrashim. Some of the midrashim are based solely on the meaning of a word, whether that meaning comes from scholarly sources, Rabbinic sources, or—in rare cases—modern usage. Others are based on how an individual word is used in the context of a particular moment in Torah.

Approach and Interpretation

Most of the Torah research was conducted online (see the Bibliographic Essay at the end of this volume). The definitions generally follow Ernest Klein's *A Comprehensive Etymological Dictionary of the Hebrew Language for Readers of English* but occasionally will include entries from other dictionaries. The focus is on biblical definitions, although at times there will be references to postbiblical or Modern Hebrew translations, identified in the text. To facilitate readability, single quotation marks are used for definitions/translations of individual words and phrases; all other quotes use double quotation marks. References to the Talmud are from the *Bavli*, the Babylonian Talmud, unless otherwise noted. Passages from Torah are from Rabbi W. Gunther Plaut's *The Torah: A Modern Commentary*, revised edition, unless otherwise noted.

Hebrew verbs derive primarily from three-letter roots. While there are also some four-letter roots, they occur mainly in Modern Hebrew. Verb roots are often the building blocks of nouns and adjectives. There are some Sages—notably Rashi—who employ two- and one-letter stems for creating meaning or etymological connections between words. While using two-letter roots seems like a perfectly reasonable approach for developing midrash, drawing on stems to make an etymological case for a connection between words is a challenge. As a result, I have generally avoided this approach.

This volume occasionally refers to interpretations based on three approaches: *g'matria*, *notarikon*, and *t'murah*. *G'matria* applies the numeric values of each Hebrew letter. By summing the values—and other mathematical hijinks, like adding one for the word itself—*g'matria* is used to create connections between words and concepts. *Notarikon* breaks a word or set of words into individual letters—using first or final letters—to stand for another word, to form a new sentence, or to tease out an idea from the word. *T'murah* is the systematic swapping of letters to create new meanings.

Two other important topics: First, Hebrew is a gendered language. I do not shy away from addressing gender-conscious interpretation, nor do I seek to illuminate it as a particular goal. However, recognizing the challenges of anthropomorphizing God, in two cases for which a male verb describes the action of the Deity, *vayipach* and *vayikra*, the translations are purposefully gender-neutral. Second, in researching and writing this book, I took the classic view of Torah as God's singular work. As a result, I didn't explore how—or if—authorship theories such as the documentary hypothesis might impact my understanding of a word for purposes of poetic interpretation. This view is consistent with that of the Sages of old who are quoted in this volume.

How to Use This Book

These Words is written for rabbis, clergy, Jewish professionals, lay leaders, and congregants alike. I hope you will find poetic, liturgical, and spiritual resonance in its pages. The poems build on the tradition of adding a modern voice to ancient yearnings as reflected in my CCAR Press trilogy, *This Grateful Heart: Psalms and Prayers for a New Day*, *This Joyous Soul: A New Voice for Ancient Yearnings*, and *This Precious Life:*

Encountering the Divine with Poetry and Prayer. These Words was written to be read and enjoyed for its poetry.

Along with the poetry, the background on each word opens a variety of additional potential uses, including the following:

- Reading during worship services
- Individual study of the weekly Torah portion
- Torah study in congregational Shabbat *parashah* discussion groups
- Writing *divrei Torah*
- Use in adult education programming
- Use in teen and youth religious school education
- Interfaith dialogue
- Study in conversion programs
- Clergy counseling with congregants
- Hebrew language instruction

The chapter introductions add more Torah to the volume, but their primary purpose is to illuminate how the words fit with each other in that chapter. To increase the utility of the book, we have included an alphabetical index.

Yours Now

My soul has always yearned for Hebrew. Perhaps yours does, as well. The soul cannot be denied. My hope is that your soul will find meaning in *These Words*, that your soul will yearn for even more words of Torah. I invite you to dig deeper into each word, drawing interpretations of your own. These words are yours now, as they've always been, words given to us all.

As for me, well, this book is my answer to my decades-old question: Can I learn to read Hebrew? More precisely, how hard am I willing to work for Hebrew? How hard am I willing to work to get some Torah? How hard am I willing to work in service to God's holy name?

These Words

God

𖤍

וַיֹּאמֶר מֹשֶׁה אֶל־הָאֱלֹהִים הִנֵּה אָנֹכִי בָא אֶל־בְּנֵי יִשְׂרָאֵל
וְאָמַרְתִּי לָהֶם אֱלֹהֵי אֲבוֹתֵיכֶם שְׁלָחַנִי אֲלֵיכֶם וְאָמְרוּ־לִי
מַה־שְּׁמוֹ מָה אֹמַר אֲלֵהֶם:

Moses said to God, "When I come to the Israelites and say to them,
'The God of your ancestors has sent me to you,' and they ask me,
'What is [God's] name?' what shall I say to them?"
—Exodus 3:13

WE BEGIN BEFORE THE BEGINNING, with the One who existed before
existence, with an exploration of some of God's names, as well as
two other words about our relationship to the Creator. These words
include three of the seven names that, once written, cannot be erased:
Elohim, Adonai, and *El.* The others that cannot be erased, listed in Maimonides's *Mishneh Torah, Hilchot Y'sodei HaTorah* 6, are *Elo-ah, Elohai,
El Shaddai,* and *Tz'vaot.* We'll also explore *Ehyeh* (I will be), perhaps
the most enigmatic of God's names. Our exploration concludes with
Anochi (I)—a poetic form of the first-person reference—and *Echad*
(One), which captures the singularity of God and our spiritual goal of
unifying all of God's names, reflected in the *Sh'ma.*

According to the midrash (*Sh'mot Rabbah* 3:6), God explained the
meanings of the divine names to Moses:

> God said to Moses, "You wish to know My name; I am called accord-
> ing to My deeds. Sometimes I am called *El Shaddai, Tz'vaot, Elohim,
> Adonai.* When I judge Creation, I'm called *Elohim.* When I am waging
> war against the wicked, I'm called *Tz'vaot* [God of Hosts]. When I
> suspend punishment for sin, I'm called *El Shaddai* [God Almighty].
> When I am merciful toward My world, I'm called *Adonai,* for *Adonai*
> only refers to the attribute of mercy, as it is said: '*Adonai, Adonai,*
> God, merciful and gracious' [Exodus 34:6]. Hence, *Ehyeh Asher Ehyeh*
> [I will be that I will be], I am called according to My deeds."

אֱלֹהִים
Elohim, God

THE FIRST CHAPTER of Genesis leaves no room to question who created heaven and earth: *Elohim*, God. The name *Elohim* appears thirty-two times in the chapter's thirty-one verses. God is without question the Creator. Yet as certain as the Torah is about who created the universe, it leaves unanswered questions about God's first revealed name.

Elohim is alternatively used in the Torah to mean not only the One God of the Hebrews, but also gods in general; supernatural or super-human beings; angels; rulers or judges; a human with godlike power or authority; works of God; or things specifically belonging to God. When *Elohim* takes a singular pronoun, it always means the One.

The word's root and etymology are also in question. Some scholars see *Elohim* as the plural of *El*, with the infix of the letter *hei*. Other scholars question whether *Elohim* is the plural of *Elo-ah*. Or perhaps *Elo-ah* is a back formation from *Elohim*.

Elohim is the name of God associated with the natural order of the universe. *Elohim* totals eighty-six in *g'matria*, the same as *hateva*, 'nature.' The laws of nature are constant and impersonal. There are times when God relies solely on natural law, which the Rabbis equate with justice. Moreover, as a plural that takes a singular pronoun, *Elohim* might imply the royal 'we.' *Elohim* can be split into *el hayam*. With *hayam* as 'the sea,' *el hayam* might allude to the Egyptians pursuing the Israelites at the Red Sea. Gods shows strict justice when the Egyptians are destroyed in the sea. The Rabbis say that the world could not exist without God's justice, but it can't survive with only justice. In the second chapter of Genesis, the Creator is called *Adonai Elohim*, representing both justice and mercy.

Everything

Everything was God,
Until God created everything.

Chaos, unformed,
Shapeless nothing,
God fashioned order from the void.

Vibrant darkness,
Dense brilliance,
Indistinguishable,
God extracted day from night.

One day after another,
God created the rules
That govern the universe.
Physics, chemistry, biology,
The laws of nature and life
That do not bend,
The strict justice
That protects everything
From returning
To chaos.

יהוה
Adonai, God

ONE DAY A YEAR—on Yom Kippur in the Holy of Holies—the High Priest pronounced God's intimate, personal name. That was two thousand years ago. Since then, we have stopped using the true pronunciation, and it is apparently lost. As a people, we have forgotten how to say the most powerful and sacred name of God ever revealed to us. A stunning loss. Instead, we pronounce the four letters of the Tetragrammaton as *Adonai* and ascribe the same respect to it as if we were actually speaking God's name. We are so accustomed to not knowing God's name that the fact that we forgot it is no longer startling to us.

The exclusive use of *yod-hei-vav-hei* by the High Priest didn't begin until the Second Temple period. According to *Tosefta Sotah* 11:8, "Since the death of Shimon the Tzaddik, they stopped blessing in the Name." In other words, before the time of the High Priest Simeon the Just, about 300 BCE, priests blessed the people speaking the Tetragrammaton. Legend says that to this day, there are a few Jews in every generation who know the precise pronunciation.

Translating *Adonai* is a challenge. In the English text in *The Torah: A Women's Commentary*, the Tetragrammaton appears as the four Hebrew letters without vowels, avoiding the issue of translation. The Stone commentary similarly avoids translation, but uses 'HASHEM' in the English text. The Plaut alternatively uses 'Eternal' and 'Eternal One,' while other translations across the Jewish spectrum use the more traditional 'Lord.' *The Living Torah* renders *Adonai* as 'God.' *Adonai* is associated with God's *midat rachamim*, the attribute of mercy. The Tetragrammaton ends with a *hei*, which can indicate a feminine noun. Thus, the feminine aspect of God is hinted by the *hei* ending of the Tetragrammaton, which first appears in Torah in Genesis when Adam is created (Genesis 2:4).

The letters *yod-hei-vav-hei* comprise the past, the present, and the future tenses of the verb 'to be': *hayah*, 'was'; *hoveh*, 'is'; and *yihyeh*, 'will be.' God encompasses all of time simultaneously, therefore transcending time.

Secret Name

Above time
       Below time
Beyond time
       Within time
All of time
       At the same time
Timeless
       Without time
Sustaining time
       With mercy.

Do You miss
Hearing Your name
In the prayers
Of Your people?
Or are You waiting for those
Who have surrendered Your invitation
To know You by name
To return and to call out to You
In blessing,
With love?

Perhaps You whisper
Your name to us
In dreams.

Perhaps You
Have also
Forgotten.

Or perhaps You are
Simply waiting
For us to ask.

אֵל

El, God

As the *T'filah*—the *Amidah*—opens, we declare, as Moses did, "*Ha-El hagadol hagibor v'hanora*," "The great, the mighty, and the awesome God" (Deuteronomy 10:17).

El is the name for God that connotes power and might. It's often used in conjunction with one or more adjectives in our prayers and at times in Torah. The etymology is uncertain, with some scholars arguing that it is derived from the root *alef-vav-lamed*, meaning 'to be strong' or 'to be in front.' Others maintain it's from *alef-lamed-hei*, 'to strive or reach after a person,' which Klein says would mean the one 'whom everyone strives to reach.' Others use the same *alef-lamed-hei* base to mean 'to be strong.' None of these etymologies nor any others suggested, Klein argues, is convincing, opening a variety of paths for midrashic exploration.

In praising God, neither Jeremiah nor Daniel used the full Mosaic declaration from Deuteronomy. Jeremiah, who witnessed the destruction of the First Temple omitted *nora*, 'awesome' (Jeremiah 32:18). Where is awe, when God allows heathens to sacrifice in the Temple? Daniel, who lived as Nebuchanezzar's prisoner in exile, omitted *gibor* in his praise. He does not ascribe mightiness to God, not when God's people are enslaved (Daniel 9:4).

The Rabbis of the Talmud ask: How can these two prophets "uproot the teaching of Moses?" (*Yoma* 69b). Rabbi Elazar said that they did so because they knew God as truthful. Consequently, they did not speak falsely about God. Jeremiah did not experience God's awesomeness. Daniel did not experience God's might. Even as we use the full Mosaic formula in our prayers, we call out to the God of our experience, the God of our own understanding.

El is both a prefix and a suffix in many Hebrew names, like Samuel, Israel, Elkanah, and Elisheva. It appears with only one pronominal suffix, a *yod*, yielding *Eli*, 'my God,' used in songs both old and new. Perhaps the most famous popular use is in the poem "A Walk to Caesarea" by Hannah Szenes, known by the opening words "*Eli, Eli*" and set to music by Israeli composer David Zehavi in 1945.

A Psalm of Names

Eli, Eli,
My God, my God,
You are Almighty, overflowing with Abundance;
You are Benevolent, overflowing with Blessing.
The Creator, sustaining life with Compassion,
You are Destiny, the source of Delight;
Exalted, Existence itself,
Father of Forgiveness,
Gracious and full of Glory,
Healer and Help,
Immense and Immanent,
Judge and Justice,
Kindness and King,
Love and Light,
Mother of Mercy,
Noble and Never-ending,
The One,
Pardoner, Protector,
Quintessential Queen,
Rock and Refuge,
Source and Shepard,
Tender Teacher, Transcendent and True,
Ultimate, Unbound, the Universe,
Virtue and Vastness,
Whispers and Wisdom,
Yearning for Your people,
The Zenith of all.

You are the God beyond perception,
The God beyond understanding,
Who answered our ancestors,
Our Hope and our Salvation.

אֶהְיֶה
Ehyeh, I Will Be

EHYEH—'I WILL BE'—is perhaps the most perplexing and beautiful of all the names that God calls Godself. It appears as God's name only in the story of the burning bush: Moses asks God, "When [the people] ask me, 'What is [God's] name?' what shall I say to them?" God responds, "*Ehyeh-Asher-Ehyeh*," continuing, "Thus shall you say to the Israelites, '*Ehyeh* sent me to you'" (Exodus 3:13–14).

The Talmud (*B'rachot* 9b), noticing that the instruction to say *Ehyeh-Asher-Ehyeh* changes immediately to the single name *Ehyeh*, explains: In the double use, the first *Ehyeh* is God saying, "I will be with the people in this sorrow," and the second *Ehyeh* is God saying, "I will be with them in future sufferings." Moses says to God, "Why should I mention other sorrows? They have enough with this sorrow!" God replies, "You have spoken rightly, thus say *Ehyeh*, 'I am.'"

The midrash (*Sh'mot Rabbah* 3:6) takes a different tack, concluding that each *Ehyeh* has a separate meaning: "I am the One who has been, the One who is now, and the One who will be in the future." This is implied by *Ehyeh*'s root *hei-vav-hei* meaning 'to be, exist, happen, become,' essentially the verb 'to be,' the same root as the Tetragrammaton.

Ramban thinks something more profound is revealed in this name of God. Moses understood that the people would want to know which of God's attributes would be present for them in their liberation and destiny. Rabbi Jordan D. Cohen explains, "The name *Ehyeh-Asher-Ehyeh* teaches us that God will be with the people of Israel in the same way as the people will be with God. If the people are giving, God will be giving. If the people are not giving, then God will not be giving."

Rabbi Peter Knobel put it this way: "I believe God said something like the following, 'I am whatever you want Me to be. I am whatever you need Me to be. You cannot know My essence, but we will have a relationship, and you will tell stories about your encounters with Me. None of them will be totally accurate because I am not a concept. I am a living complex reality that can be experienced, but not defined or limited by language. That is Who I Am and Who I Will Be.'"

Ehyeh

I will be with you when you open Your heart to Me,
Just as I was before,
In the ancient days,
When your mothers and fathers
Discovered Me.

How many invitations
Do you need
To holiness
And redemption?

My love
Can't be fully counted
By you,
Like the stars in the heavens,
Try as you may.
And My secrets
Cannot be fully known
By you,
Like the whispers in the breeze,
Try as you may.

How many names
Will you create for Me,
Before your heart understands,
I am
That I am,
That I am,
That I am.

אָנֹכִי
Anochi, I

THE TEN COMMANDMENTS begin with a first-person personal pronoun: *Anochi Adonai Elohecha*, "I am *Adonai* your God" (Exodus 20:2).
All of Torah hinges on knowing and recognizing that *Adonai* is God.

Adam is the first to use the word *anochi*. When God asks in the Garden of Eden, "Where are you?" Adam answers, "I was afraid because
I was naked, so I hid myself" (Genesis 3:9–10). Cain employs *anochi*
when answering God: "Am I my brother's keeper?" (4:9). God uses this
personal pronoun in telling Noah, "I will pour rain upon the earth for
forty days and nights" (7:4). When Abraham argues with God to save
Sodom and Gomorrah, he uses *anochi*, saying, "I am dust and ashes"
(18:27). Both God and Moses refer to themselves with *anochi* during
their encounter at the Burning Bush (Exodus 3:6, 3:11).

Anochi is one of two Hebrew first-person personal pronouns, the
other being *ani*. Both of their dictionary definitions are remarkably simple. They are pure synonyms until the Rabbis begin to wonder if there is
a distinction. Malbim and Shadal say that *anochi* has an added emphasis of 'I *and* not others.' Rav Samson Raphael Hirsch goes further,
saying that *anochi* proclaims the speaker as intimately near to the one
addressed. *Anochi* comprehends, bears, and keeps the one addressed.
From *anochi* the one addressed gets personal existence and standing.

The conclusion that there is a deeper significance to the word *anochi*
centers on the divine use of the word for Godself. The Talmud (*Shabbat*
105a) says that when used in the Ten Commandments, the letters of *anochi*—*alef, nun, chaf, yod*—are an acronym for three alternative phrases.
The first tells us that God gave the Torah: *Ana nafshi k'tivat y'havit*, 'I
Myself wrote and gave it,' alternatively translated as 'I placed My soul
in the text.' The second teaches that the words of the Torah are pleasant: *Amirah n'imah k'tivah y'hivah*, 'A pleasant statement was written and
given.' The third is based on interpreting the letters in reverse order,
asserting the faithfulness of Torah: *Y'hivah k'tivah ne-emanim amareha*,
'It was written, it was given, its statements are faithful.'

The Intimate I

I, the intimate I,
The I that leans toward you
To whisper,
In faith and joy,
The I that holds we
In its eyes,
Is the I that holds love and longing,
The I that carries
My heart to yours.

The I,
The intimate I,
The one that yearns for the intimate we,
Is the we that carries
Hope and wisdom between us,
The we that is faithful and true,
The we that carries
Warmth and pleasantness
From my heart to yours.

אֶחָד
Echad, One

PERHAPS THE MOST FAMOUS use of the word *echad* in all of Jewish life is at the end of the *Sh'ma* (Deuteronomy 4:6). *Echad* means 'one, single,' and at times 'first, someone.' It comes from the root *yod-chet-dalet*, or *yachad*, meaning 'to be one, to make one, to unite.'

Echad is a riddle. Rambam says that God's oneness is unique, unlike any kind of unity or whole that humans can experience, an "incomparable oneness" beyond our ability to grasp. The *Zohar* states that God "fills and surrounds all worlds"; *Tikkunei HaZohar* claims that "God is everything, and everything is God." All is part of One, and God, also according to Kabbalah, is the *Ein Sof*, the One without End, the existence before existence.

The *g'matria* of *echad* is thirteen. One explanation is that *alef*, with a value of one, represents the One God; the *chet*, with a value of eight, represents the covenant of circumcision after eight days; and the *dalet*, with a value of four, represents the future acceptance of *Adonai* as God throughout the four corners of the earth. Other interpretations hold that the *dalet* represents the four cardinal directions or the four basic elements: earth, air, fire, and water.

Echad is also the riddle of the *Sh'ma*. In that six-word declaration, we use two names to proclaim One God: *Adonai* and *Elohim*. In doing so, according to the Sages, we are unifying God's names. Note that the last letter of the word *echad* is enlarged in sacred text, just as the last letter of the first word of the line, the word *sh'ma*, is enlarged. Together, the enlarged *ayin* of *sh'ma* and the enlarged *dalet* of the word *echad* form the word *ad* (eternity). God is the Eternal. The root of the word *ad*—*alef-vav-dalet*—also means 'witness, testimony.' We are God's witnesses.

One beyond Understanding

You'd think
That the number one
Would be easy
To understand.
Simple. Singular. One.

Turns out
That the number one
Can be everything
Or nothing.
Unknowable. Unreachable. Unfathomable.

You are the One,
The everything
That I'm not,
And the nothing
That includes me.
The eternity and
The without end.
The existence beyond existence.

Let us rejoice
In knowing
And not knowing
The Indivisible One,
In witnessing
The One that is beyond imagining,
The One that is all of everything.

Creation

❦

בְּרֵאשִׁית בָּרָא אֱלֹהִים אֵת הַשָּׁמַיִם וְאֵת הָאָרֶץ:
וְהָאָרֶץ הָיְתָה תֹהוּ וָבֹהוּ וְחֹשֶׁךְ עַל־פְּנֵי תְהוֹם
וְרוּחַ אֱלֹהִים מְרַחֶפֶת עַל־פְּנֵי הַמָּיִם:

When God was about to create heaven and earth,
the earth was a chaos, unformed,
and on the chaotic waters' face there was darkness.
Then God's spirit glided over the face of the waters.
—Genesis 1:1–2

BEFITTING THE MYSTERY that is Creation, the story of the beginning is punctuated with mysterious language. The word *b'reishit* (in beginning)—also the Hebrew name for the Book of Genesis—is a grammatical puzzle. The mysterious language continues with *shamayim* (heavens), *tohu vavohu* (chaos, unformed), *or* (light), and *rakiya* (firmament). Each adds a mystique to the story, simultaneously illuminating the process of Creation and adding complexity to the tale. These words call out to be reexamined in usage, etymology, and grammatical structure. Our exploration of Creation includes the events in the Garden of Eden through the words *shamor* (keep), *nachash* (snake), and *kedem* (east).

According to the Talmud (*P'sachim* 54a), seven phenomena were brought into being before the world was created: Torah, repentance, the Garden of Eden, Gehenna (purgatory), the Throne of Glory, the Temple, and the name of the Messiah. Even Creation has a backstory. The words in this section begin to unravel the story behind the story of Creation.

בְּרֵאשִׁית
B'reishit, In Beginning

THE FIRST WORD of the Torah—the name of its first book, *B'reishit*—begins our journey with a mystery (Genesis 1:1). It confounds grammar and serves as a jumping-off point for commentary. No single, simple translation is adequate to understand it.

B'reishit is the word *reishit* with the prepositional prefix *bet*, or 'in.' *Reishit* means 'beginning, first fruits, choicest parts.' Together, they yield 'in beginning.' *B'reishit* is in the construct form—known as a noun pair—which means that it should be immediately connected to another noun, yet in the text it is followed by a verb. The conflict between the form of the word and the actual sentence structure opens a door to differences and disagreements in translation and interpretation. This grammatical anomaly underscores the idea that Creation is a mystery.

Sforno teaches that *b'reishit* means 'in the beginning of time.' He says that this is when time, previously an 'unbroken continuity,' was first divisible into periods. Baal HaTurim notes that the numeric value of *bet* is two, indicating that God created both a Written Torah and an Oral Law. Other commentators focus on the meaning of *reishit* as 'first fruits,' implying that the purpose of Creation is to create the opportunity for Jews to dedicate first fruits—their intial efforts and successes—to God.

The odd structure leads to conflicting translations of the opening phrase *B'reishit bara Elohim*, such as 'In the beginning God created' (Soncino) and 'When God was about to create' (Plaut). The former translation implies that God created the universe *ex nihilo*, from nothing. The latter is based on Rashi's assertion that the word should have been written *barishonah*, 'at first.'

Rabbi Jeffrey W. Goldwasser says that *b'reishit*, in construct form without another noun as pair, might be thought of as paired with itself, interpreting the phrase to mean "In the beginning of the beginning that is always beginning, God created the creation that is still [that endures]."

Evidence of Mysteries

Suppose God
Plays hide and seek
Among the stars,
Leaving evidence of holiness
In the heavens,
So that we might yearn
To glimpse the moment when
The divine desire to create
Burst forth
Into an explosion of awe and wonder.

Suppose God
Plays hide and seek
Among the words of Torah,
From the beginning of the beginning,
Leaving evidence of mysteries
In the text,
So that we might yearn
To glimpse deeper wonders
Of divine revelation
Bursting forth
From the beginning of time.

שָׁמַיִם
Shamayim, Heavens

ENGLISH TEXTS of the Torah are split on whether to translate *shamayim* as 'heaven' or 'sky,' often switching between them depending on context. The first usage is most commonly translated as 'heavens' (Genesis 1:1). The word is pivotal in the stories of Creation, the Tower of Babel (11:1–9), and of the Flood (6:5–9:28).

Shamayim—which has no singular form—can mean both 'visible heaven, sky,' as well as 'heaven, abode of God.' Klein associates it with a variety of words from earlier languages—such as the Ethiopian *samay*, and the Akkadian *shamū*—with the original meaning of each likely being 'high place, height.'

The early Rabbis broke *shamayim* into two parts, attempting to find hidden meanings in the word based on the Hebrew word for water, *mayim*. Rashi offers three possible interpretations, each a wordplay and each with its own linguistic issue: *sham mayim*, *sa mayim*, and *eish umayim*. Ramban says that there's a *mem* missing from the word, noting that at times in Hebrew spelling, one letter can represent two instances of the same letter appearing consecutively. In such cases, one of the duplicate letters drops out and is typically represented by the addition or change of a vowel. Adding back the "missing" *mem*, the result would be *sham mayim*, 'there [in that place] is water.'

In *Siftei Chachamim*, Shabbetai ben Joseph Bass explains that Rashi is reading the *shin* of *shamayim* as the letter *sin*, yielding *sa mayim*, 'carry water.' He points out that the vowel *kamatz* is beneath the original *shin*. He says that the *kamatz* allows for the letter *alef*, so he adds one, to complete *sa mayim*. Reversing the order of the *alef* and the *shin*, yields *eish umayim*, 'fire and water.'

According to *B'reishit Rabbah* 4:7 and the Talmud (*Chagigah* 12a), God mixed fire and water to create the heavens, with that secret hidden in the letter-scramble of *eish umayim* becoming *shamayim* in our text. Thus, according to Radak, *shamayim* is the place where fire and water coexist. As a result of oppsites dwelling in harmony, Kli Yakar says that the word *shamayim* indicates peace.

Contrasts

Isn't it strange
There is no justice without mercy
And no mercy without justice?

Isn't it strange
There is no joy without sorrow
And no sorrow without joy?

Isn't it strange
There is no holy without the mundane
And no mundane without holiness?

Stranger still
To know that our hearts and souls
Can hold it all,
The endless darkness
And the eternal light,
The fire and the water
Of life itself.

תֹהוּ וָבֹהוּ
Tohu Vavohu, Chaos, Unformed

THE PRIMORDIAL STATE of existence, as God began to create the universe, is described as *tohu vavohu* (Genesis 1:2), a phrase that has yielded a wide variety of translations, such as 'unformed and void'; 'astonishingly empty'; 'without form and empty'; and 'chaos, unformed.'

Each word has a variety of definitions as well. Klein defines *tohu* as 'emptiness, waste, desert, chaos, confusion,' but also as 'vanity, nothingness, worthlessness.' The Brown, Driver, Briggs (BDB) dictionary defines *tohu* as 'formlessness, confusion, unreality, emptiness.' Klein pegs the root as *tav-vav-hei*, meaning 'to be astonished, astounded, amazed.' Both Klein and the BDB define *vohu* as 'emptiness,' with Klein adding 'chaos.' Klein links this to the root *bet-hei-hei*, also meaning 'to be astonished, amazed.'

The rabbis attempt to make sense out of this enigmatic phrase. Sforno says that *tohu* relates to the mixture of raw materials from which the universe was created, while *vohu* describes the external appearance of the universe in that moment. *Tohu*, he says, indicates that this 'unformed emptiness' was potential that had not yet materialized. Rabbeinu Bachya says *tohu vavohu* refers to the raw material created by God to be used for Creation, which had not yet been properly defined and could not yet be named. *Siftei Chachamim* quotes the translation of *tohu vavohu* in *Targum Onkelos*: 'desolation and empty space.' In other words, *tohu vavohu* are the raw materials of Creation.

Another word later in the same passage, *t'hom*, echoes the sound of the word *tohu*. Klein defines *t'hom* as 'deep, abyss, sea'; many Torah commentaries translate it as 'the deep.' Shadal says *t'hom* "is an expression of disorientation and wonderment, except that it is used specifically about the abundance of waters and their depth."

The Torah relates, "The earth was a chaos, unformed, and on the chaotic waters' face there was darkness. Then God's spirit glided over the face of the waters" (Genesis 1:2). The image is frightening. Yet from this, all of Creation comes into being.

At the Edge of the Deep

In a dream,
God took me to the swamp,
The formless deep,
Roiling with anticipation and desire,
From which divine yearning
Created us all.

Everything held in nothingness,
Light confined in darkness.
Life calling out in song,
Souls calling out in prayer.
Seeds of beauty and terror,
Seeds of history and eternity.

God asked me:
"Shall we make Human in our own image?"
Confused, I replied, "You've already made me."
"Oh, dear one," God said,
"Before I created you
You called out to Me from the deep,
You yearned for Me,
You courted Me,
And I fell in love."

אוֹר
Or, Light

ON THE FIRST DAY of Creation, God creates light. The word for 'light' is *or*, also meaning 'brightness, daylight.' *Or* is used five times on the first day of Creation (Genesis 1:3–5). In the Talmud (*Chagigah* 12a), the Rabbis assert that the light created on the first day is fundamentally different from the light that comes from the luminaries—the sun, moon, and stars—which are created on the fourth day (1:14–15).

The light created on the first day allowed humanity to see from one end of the world to the other, according to the Sages. God, realizing that this spiritual light might be misused, conceals it for use in a future time only by the righteous. The *Zohar* says that every day a ray from that hidden light, the *or haganuz*, emanates into the world to sustain all of Creation.

The root for 'light,' *alef-vav-reish*, means 'to give light, shine.' Another word with the same root is used five times in the Creation story, on the fourth day: *maor*, 'luminary' (*mem-alef-vav-reish*). Treating the *mem* as a prefix to *or* yields 'from light.' So, the luminaries are from light, but which light? Kli Yakar answers: the *mem* indicates that God took a sliver from the spiritual light created on the first day to imbue the luminaries with the physical light that we experience.

That spiritual light, the Rabbis assert, is also hidden in Torah. In *B'reishit Rabbah* 3:5, Rabbi Shimon says that the five instances of the word *or* on the first day of Creation correspond to the five books of Torah. According to the *Zohar*, in every place that Torah is studied into the night, a sliver of *or haganuz* enters the world, flowing to those who study in order to sustain Torah learning. There's another tradition that the *or haganuz* is also stored in the lights kindled on Chanukah.

Light Leaks

In the darkest dark,
With a sky full of stars,
As the Milky Way
Arches across the heavens,
My heart remembers
The moment of Creation.

Light cannot be concealed,
Not even by God,
Not even that special light
Reserved only for the righteous.
It leaks out from the vaults of heaven
Into the words of Torah
To guide our way.

The light is yours,
When you seek it with your heart.
The heart that's inside your soul,
The heart that's inside your breathing,
The heart that's inside your being.

In the brightest brightness,
In a day full of light,
As the sun travels
Across a full-moon sky,
My heart remembers
God's blessings.

רָקִיעַ
Rakiya, Firmament

OUR PLANET, according to scientists, is surrounded by a faint multicolored glow known as airglow, a phenomenon of the upper atmosphere. It marks the border between space and earth.

On the second day of Creation, God creates the *rakiya*, the 'firmament, expanse,' in the midst of the waters, separating the 'upper waters' from the 'lower waters' (Genesis 1:6–7). God names the expanse *shamayim*, 'heaven, sky' (1:8). The next day, God gathers the waters beneath the heavens, and dry land appears (1:9). On the fourth day, God places the sun, moon, and stars into the expanse of sky (1:14). The following day God creates birds that fly above the earth and across the expanse of the sky (1:20). This is the last of the nine times *rakiya* is mentioned in the Torah.

Rakiya, which also means 'extended surface, sky,' comes from the root *reish-kof-ayin*, meaning 'stamp, beat out, spread out [by hammering].' *Rakiya* is associated with the Jewish Palestinian Aramaic word *arka*, 'he spread out,' and the Phoenician *mrakah*, 'platter of gold.' Various rabbis in *B'reishit Rabbah* 4:2 imagine the *rakiya* as a thin beaten surface made solid by fire—gleaming, perhaps like airglow.

The Rabbis did not envision the *rakiya* as surrounding a globe. In their flat-earth cosmography, with a dome-shaped *rakiya*, it might be possible to find the place where heaven and earth meet. In a Talmudic legend (*Bava Batra* 74a), an Arab takes Rabbah bar bar Chanah to the place where the earth and the heavens touch. "I took my basket and placed it in a window of the heavens," Rabbah bar bar Chanah says. The Rabbis dismiss him as telling a foolish tale, but only because in their estimation it would be an impossibly long walk.

Why did God rename the *rakiya* as *shamayim*? Kli Yakar explains that 'firmament' represents division and disagreement, so God chose a different name that means 'peace.'

Heaven Meets Earth

I took my basket
And went to look
For the place
Where heaven and earth
Touch.

I took an apple, a pear,
And a loaf of hard-crusted bread.
I took jam and water,
My curious hope,
And a question that could not be answered.

I took my heart
And went to look
For the place
Where the radiance of eternity
Shines.

Dear friend,
Come with me
And ride in the firmament of heaven.
Ride with me on the glow of Creation.
Let's walk together on the solid earth,
And we will find
The place where our lives
And God's shelter
Meet.

שָׁמוֹר
Shamor, Keep

GOD BRINGS ADAM into the Garden of Eden "to work it and to keep it" (Genesis 2:15). *Shamor* is the imperative form of the word 'keep,' derived from the root *shin-mem-reish* meaning 'keep, heed, watch over, guard, observe.' Depending on context, Torah commentaries switch between 'keep' and 'guard' in translating *shamor*.

When God inquires of Cain about the fate of his brother Abel, Cain asks, "Am I my brother's keeper?" (Genesis 4:9). Abraham and the generations that follow are instructed to keep the covenant of circumcision (17:9–10). Repeatedly, the Israelites are instructed to 'keep' the Sabbath (e.g., Exodus 31:16; Deuteronomy 5:12).

Ibn Ezra and Chizkuni, on the meaning of 'guard' to describe the task given to Adam in the Garden, wonder why it would need protection. They reason that the Garden needed to be guarded from wild animals entering Eden and trampling it.

Chizkuni offers an alternative exegesis of the phrase "to work it and to keep it"—*l'ovdah ul'shomrah* (Genesis 2:15)—based on his conclusion that the Sabbath was observed in the Garden. *L'ovdah* (to work), he says, matches the command to confine work to six days—"Six days shall you labor and do all your work"—by using the same root for 'work' in the verse in the form of *taavod* (Exodus 20:9). To 'keep' the garden, *ul'shomrah*, matches the command to 'keep' the Sabbath found in the second presentation of the Ten Commandments, *shamor* (Deuteronomy 5:12). "In other words," Chizkuki writes, "God commanded Adam at that time to observe the seventh day of the week as Jews were commanded to observe the Sabbath after the Torah had been given—by not performing work on that day."

Ironically, once Adam and Eve are expelled from the Garden, it needs to be protected from human reentry. God places a whirling, flaming sword and cherubim on the path to Eden to guard it, again a form of the word *shamor*.

Uncle Izzy

Uncle Izzy
Used to tell us
Stories of Shabbat
In the Garden
As if he'd been there himself.

"We lit candles by the orchid blossoms."
"The grape vines poured out wine for *Kiddush*."
"The birds sang *z'mirot* with us."
"The trees bowed when the Sabbath Queen arrived."

No one believed him,
Of course,
Except him,
But that was enough
To make us wonder—
We, the children who
Loved the way he told tales—
If maybe,
Just maybe,
He knew a secret passageway,
Hidden from the cherubim,
Safe from the flaming sword,
Back to a place
Where the beauty of Creation
And the holiness of Shabbat
Could meet again.

בָּחָשׁ
Nachash, Serpent

TORAH IS CRAWLING with snakes. Snakes are signs of God's power to both Moses and Pharaoh (Exodus 4:2–4, 7:9–12). God sends a plague of snakes against the Israelites for speaking against God and Moses (Numbers 21:4–9). Perhaps best known among the biblical snakes is the wily talking creature who tempted Eve in the Garden (Genesis 3:1–7).

There's little to say about the etymology of the word for snake, *nachash*. Klein offers that it is likely related to the Arabic word for serpent, *hanash*. David Curwin explains that this would be a case of metathesis, a language pattern in which a sequence of two sounds occurs in one order in one context and in the opposite order in a related context. *Nachash* may be onomatopoetic, with a root of the hissing sound of *chash*, but there are no primary sources to support the idea.

Commentators hold a wide range of views on the moral culpability of the snake in the Garden. Sforno and Rabbeinu Bachya see the snake as the devil incarnate. But Saadyah Gaon and Chizkuni—who say that the snake's speech was animated by an angel of God, just as Balaam's donkey spoke by virtue of an angel (Numbers 22:28)—minimize the blame. In contrast, Ibn Ezra holds that the snake was morally responsible, since it walked upright and could speak.

In the desert, the Israelites complain about Moses and Aaron multiple times; then they complain about God and God's gift of manna in the wilderness (Numbers 21:5). This lack of gratitude brings a plague of snakes. Rashi says the snakebites caused a burning fever from which one could not recover. Many died. When the people repent, God tells Moses to make the copper serpent; whoever is bitten by a snake and looks at the statue is immediately healed (21:8–9). In this one story, the serpent kills and the serpent heals. But Mishnah Rosh Hashanah 3:8 asks if a copper snake could cause life or death. It was only those with true hearts of repentance, the midrash concludes, who were healed.

Medicine and Poison

When the serpent
Bit the back of my calf
In the desert,
The poison raced toward my heart
And I prepared to die.

Somehow, I lived.
I recall a fever dream,
A bronze snake
With flashing eyes
And the light of eternity.

Poison can be medicine
In the right hands,
And medicine can kill,
But only God can offer
Salvation.

When the snake
Offered me fruit and passion
In the Garden,
The medicine raced toward my heart
And I prepared to live.

Somehow, I died.
I recall the innocence
And the wonder
Of being banished
To a place more human
And frail.

Medicine can be poison
In the wrong hands,
And poison can heal,
But only God can offer
Salvation.

קֶדֶם
Kedem, East

SOMEWHERE TO THE EAST, cherubim and a fiery spinning sword guard the entrance to the Garden of Eden (Genesis 3:24). East, where God planted the Garden, is where humanity begins our journey (2:8).

Kedem can mean 'what is in front, forward,' as well as 'east.' It's from the root *kof-dalet-mem*, which means 'to be before, be in front,' and is the same root as the postbiblical Hebrew word *kodem*, 'before.' *Kedem* is the direction from which the new day's sun appears, the land that witnesses the first sun. It is one of three words for 'east,' along with *mizrach* and *panim*.

Each of the cardinal directions has a set of three biblical words, teaches Rabbi Michael Hattin, although one of the words for north, *tzafon*, appears in two of the three sets. One set is based on the contours of the land. Another set is based on the position of the sun. The third set is based on the human body. *Mizrach* is formed from the word *zarach*—'to shine'—referring to the sun's first light. *Panim*—also the word for 'face, countenance'—does not appear in the Torah meaning 'east,' but that usage appears in other books of *Tanach*. Midrash says that when Adam was created, he was facing east. In this sense, *panim* means 'faceward.'

When God tells Abraham to look around, that his ancestors will receive all the land in every direction, the set of directions used is based on the contours of the land (Genesis 13:14–15). When God repeats that promise to Jacob, the same set is used, but in a different order (28:14). God parts the sea with a strong east wind, and the Children of Israel cross on dry land (Exodus 14:21–22).

The Torah introduces us to Eden this way: "And Adonai God planted a garden in Eden eastward" (Genesis 2:8), using the word *mikedem*, adding to *kedem* the prefix *mi-*, meaning 'from.' Reinterpreting the word *mikedem* as *mikodem*, meaning 'from before,' the Sages of the Talmud (*N'darim* 39b) assert that Eden was created before the world was created.

East/West

Creation comes from the east,
The new sun
Rising first
Over Eden
Before arriving here,
Bursting bright over our horizon,
Carrying bits
Of serenity and love,
Of tranquility and peace,
From the beginning of life
And the start of time
Into the new day.

Shechinah dwells in the west,
Guiding the light to her open heart,
Setting
The course of the sun,
And raising
The arc of eternity.

Humanity

זֶה סֵפֶר תּוֹלְדֹת אָדָם בְּיוֹם בְּרֹא אֱלֹהִים
אָדָם בִּדְמוּת אֱלֹהִים עָשָׂה אֹתוֹ:

This is the written record of the human line
from the day God created human beings,
making [them] in the likeness of God.
—Genesis 5:1

THE CREATION OF HUMANKIND is so critical that it warrants two remarkably different stories. In the first chapter of Genesis, on the sixth day, male and female are created simultaneously and are made in the image of God (Genesis 1:26–31). In the second chapter, a single human is initially created from dust, then animated with God's breath (2:7). Our lens into the creation of humanity will be through the words: *afar* (dust), *b'tzelem* (in the image), *adam* (human), and *vayipach* ([God] breathed). We'll expand our understanding of how Torah views humanity with three additional words: *tol'dot* (generations), *d'varim* (words; also the Hebrew name of the Book of Deuteronomy), and *chazak* (strong). These words connect us to the generations and hint at a vision of our best selves.

Rabbi Akiva teaches that "Love your neighbor as yourself" (Leviticus 19:18) is a major principle of the Torah, but Ben Azai says that God creating humanity in the likeness of the Divine is an even greater principle (Jerusalem Talmud, *N'darim* 9:4).

עָפָר
Afar, Dust

GOD FORMS THE FIRST HUMAN of "dust from the soil," breathing in a divine soul (Genesis 2:7). The word for dust is *afar*, whose primary meanings also include 'earth, soil' and 'debris, ashes.' The root is *ayin-pei-reish*, 'to cover with dust.'

Rabbeinu Bachya notices the repetitive language of the phrase "dust from the soil," *afar min haadamah. Afar* is a masculine noun. *Adamah* is a female noun meaning 'ground, soil, earth, land.' He says that the repetitive wording, using both masculine and feminine nouns, teaches that all earth is composed of both male and female matter. Noting that the human body contains all four elements—earth, air, fire, and water—Ibn Ezra holds that dust was used specifically to make the bones of the first human.

The Rabbis wonder: What dust did God use to create humanity? Rashi, quoting *Midrash Tanchuma*, says that to make Adam, God gathered dust from the four corners of the earth. The midrash explains the reason: so that wherever Adam might die, the ground would receive him for burial as native to that part of the land. Rashi, quoting midrash, offers another answer: God took the dust from future spot of Temple's Holy of Holies (*B'reishit Rabbah* 14:8).

God tells Abraham that his offspring will be as numerous as the stars in heaven (Genesis 26:4) and as uncountable as the dust of the earth (Genesis 13:16). Radak, quoting the *Midrash Aggadah Buber*, says that when deserving, the people are comparable to the stars in heaven, but when undeserving, they are compared to the dust of the earth. In his dream of a ladder between heaven and earth, Jacob is told by God that his descendants will be "as the dust of the earth" (Genesis 28:14). Here, the image might be that of dust in the wind, with the promise that Jacob's children would spread out in all directions.

Dust

God made
Adam
From sawdust,
And stardust,
And fairy dust,
Dust from the four corners of the earth,
Dust from the four corners of the sky,
Angel dust, moon dust,
Dust from where the rainbow ends,
Dust from Eden,
And dust from the world-to-come.
Dust that sparkles and shines,
Dust from the land where a bush
Still burns,
Waiting for you
To return
To God's holy mountain.

בְּצֶלֶם
B'tzelem, In the Image

A DIVINE LIGHT radiates from every human face, said the Maharal of Prague. A supernal spark cleaves to every human being: "In this, humanity is unique among all creations, in its radiance and in the light of the image. This light is in no way corporeal, but rather a divine, transcendent light and radiance which cleaves to humanity."

The word *b'tzelem*—'in the image'—appears only twice in the Torah and, in both cases, followed by *Elohim*. Each time the combination describes the unique nature of the creation of humankind. It is used when humanity is first created (Genesis 1:27) and again in God's blessing to Noah and his children after the Flood (9:6). Sforno says that when the name *Elohim* appears as an adjective, it refers to creatures who are spiritual in their essence, not just that they possess spiritual potential.

Without the *bet* as its propositional prefix, the word becomes *tzelem*—'image, idol, semblance'—from the Akkadian word *tzalmu*, which has the double meaning of 'image' and 'statue.' The original meaning, according to Klein, was probably 'something cut out,' as an idol cut from stone.

Humanity is created in the image of God. Rabbi Akiva does not want us to take this blessing for granted. In *Pirkei Avot*, he says that humanity is blessed twice: first, by being created in God's image, and second, in knowing that we are created in God's image.

Rav Samson Raphael Hirsch understands that being created in God's image means that humanity's physical garment—the body—is suitable to the divine purpose. "Torah teaches us to recognize and value the divine glory of the body. Indeed the Torah comes not just to sanctify the spirit, but first and foremost to sanctify the body. This is the foundation for all human morality, that the human body with all its needs and abilities was created in the image of God; and it was given to humanity to sanctify the body in a way most fit to its Divine purpose."

Divine Image

God created you,
Breathing divine breath
Into your lungs,
Into your bones,
Into your eyes.

Now the light of God's love
Can be seen in your countenance,
For the image of God,
The blessing of God,
And the radiance of God
Have been engraved
On your soul
And in your heart.

אָדָם
Adam, Human

WHEN AN *ALEF* is added to the beginning of the Hebrew word for blood, what appears is *adam*, understood in the collective sense as 'human.' *Alef*, the first letter of the alphabet, holds the numerical value of one. Mystically, the *alef* embodies the essence of the Divine. God, as we say in the *Sh'ma*, is One. From this, Rav Dov Ber, the Maggid of Mezeritch, teaches that a relationship with God is necessary for blood to attain its fullest humanity. Only those who strive for connection to the Holy One can achieve the truest human expression. With different vowels, *adam* becomes the word for red, the color of blood.

Adam is singular, meaning 'human.' In *Tanach*, *adam* is used in several generic senses: collectively (humankind), individually (a person), gender nonspecific (man or woman), and gender specific (male). *Adam* is first used as the name of a particular human in the third chapter of Genesis, after twenty-two generic uses.

The lion's share of the more than 550 uses of the word *adam* as a noun in *Tanach* are generic. It takes a singular pronoun, but in Genesis 1:27, the singular use of the word is followed by the plural pronoun in the statement that God "created them male and female." In *B'reishit Rabbah* 8:1, both Rav Shmuel bar Nachman and Reish Lakish try to reconcile the singular *adam* with the plural "them." From this grammatical discrepancy, the Rabbis teach that the first human was androgynous—half male, half female, back-to-back with separate faces, but unable to see each other or interact. Together, they are a complete human being. Rav Mike Feuer explains that since they cannot face each other, they cannot be in relationship with one another. The two halves are split by God; divine surgery separated one side of the androgynous human from the other.

Add the letter *hei* to the end of *adam* and the result is *adamah*, 'ground, soil, earth, land,' the very substance from which we are made. As a stand-alone letter, *hei* followed by an apostrophe is commonly used in lieu of God's name. With *alef* at the beginning and *hei* at the end, we might think of ourselves as blood surrounded by God, made of earth.

Blood and God

Blood
Red
Earth
God
Human
Dust and Divine
Woman-Man
Man-Woman
Split in two
In a dream
Of becoming one . . .

It takes God to make blood human.
It takes life to give God purpose.
Blood needs God.
God needs us.

וַיִּפַּח
Vayipach, [God] Breathed

GOD FORMED the first human from inert matter and then *vayipach*, 'breathed,' life into it. "God Eternal fashioned the man—dust from the soil—and breathed into his nostrils the breath of life, so that the man became a living being" (Genesis 2:7). On this verse, the *The Torah: A Women's Commentary* notes that the human being, infused with divine breath, is literally "in-spired." Humanity is the combination of dust and the Divine.

The root—*nun-pei-chet*—occurs only twelve times in all of *Tanach*, but *vayipach* is the singular use of the root in Torah and the only time it occurs in this form. The root, defined as 'blow, breathe,' is related to the Akkadian *napāḫu*, 'to inflame,' and *nappaḫu*, 'smith.' Blowing on embers can bring fire back to life. The connection between blowing, fire, and the metalsmith's use of fire come together in the second use of the root, found in Isaiah, in which God tells the prophet, "I created the smith to blow the fire of coals" (Isaiah 54:16). *Vayipach* is also related to the roots *yod-pei-chet*— to 'puff, pant, gasp'—and *pei-vav-chet*, to 'breathe, blow.'

Chizkuni reminds us that God personally blew the breath of life into the first human, something God had not done for any other creature. The *Targum Onkelos* (an Aramaic translation of the Torah) renders the phrase "so that the man became a living being" as "and the man became a speaking being."

Blowing life into Adam made the inanimate animate by providing the source of the body's functioning, including the body's temperature and our heat from within—calling to consciousness the Akkadian 'to inflame.' The gift of life from God is a gift of Godself. Quoted by both the *Zohar* and the *Tanya*, Ramban comments that one "who breathes into the nostrils of another person gives something of their own soul."

First Kiss

Part of me
Still remembers
The moment
You breathed
Life into my body,
Giving me pulse
And heartbeat,
Giving cold clay
Warmth and heat,
Giving me
A piece of Yourself,
The first kiss
Of divine love.

תּוֹלְדֹת
Tol'dot, Generations

THE FORMULA "These are the generations of" appears nine times in Genesis, creating ten sections separated by the word *tol'dot*.

Tol'dot, 'generations,' especially in the form of genealogies, are the accounts of an individual and that person's descendants, a genetic line, persons, and progeny. In its first use, however, *tol'dot* is metaphoric. "These are the generations of the heaven and of the earth when they were created" (Genesis 2:4, Soncino)—in other words, the generations of natural history.

Along with generations, *tol'dot* can mean 'history, chronology, annals, chronicles, consequences, outcomes.' Torah commentaries alternate among these definitions within their texts, based on the context. The first three uses in the Plaut employ two definitions: 'chronicle' and 'record.' The JPS uses 'story,' 'record,' and 'line' in the first three uses. The Stone uses 'products,' 'accounts,' and 'offspring.' The root of *tol'dot* is *yod-lamed-dalet*, 'to bear, bring forth, beget.' The same root can also be conjugated to mean 'children' or 'to give birth.'

Torah uses the word *tol'dot* as a marker of transitional moments in the history of humanity and the Hebrew people: the *tol'dot* of Creation (Genesis 2:4); Adam (5:1); twice for Noah and sons (6:9, 10:1); Shem (11:10); Terah (11:27); Ishmael (25:12–13); Isaac (25:19); twice for Esau (36:1,9); and Jacob (37:2). Conspicuously absent are the *tol'dot* of Abraham and Joseph. Even more conspicuously absent to our modern sensibilities: not one woman.

Or HaChayim notices that the first *tol'dot* of Noah does not follow the standard formula: "These are the generations of," followed by a genealogy. Instead, Noah's name is repeated: "These are the generations of Noah. Noah was in his generation a righteous man and whole-hearted; Noah walked with God" (Genesis 6:9, Soncino). He suggests that the pause commonly read into the text between the repetition of Noah's name is a mistake and that Noah's actions are his history. His righteous good deeds are his legacy.

Legacy

We are the generations of Eve,
   Mother of all humanity.
We are the generations of Sarah,
   Prophet of laughter and sorrow, minister to the
   Hebrew wanderers.
We are the generations of Leah, Bilhah, Zilpah, and Rachel,
   Competitors and sisters, the mothers of tribes.
We are the generations of Tamar,
   Standing for truth, the mother of kings.
We are the generations of Shiphrah and Puah,
   Midwives, saving children, the defenders of life.
We are the generations of Yocheved,
   Mother of leaders and priests.
We are the generations of Zipporah,
   Who circumcised her son and saved her husband.
We are the generations of Miriam,
   Prophet of water and song.
We are the generations of the daughters of Zelophehad—
   Mahlah, Noah, Hoglah, Milcah, and Tirzah—
   Advocates of justice.
We are the generations of Ruth, Esther, Hannah, and Devorah,
   Loyal, devoted, risk-takers.

We are the generations of unnamed women,
   Noah's wives and his son's wives, mothers of humankind.
We are the generations of unnamed women, the daughter
of Pharaoh,
   A princess, the adopted mother of a slave-child.
We are the generations of unnamed women,
   Cain's wife, Lot's wife, and Seth's daughters,
A widow living in Zarephath, Jephthah's daughter, and an
unnamed Babylonian queen.

We are the generations of named and unnamed women,
   Claiming our heritage and our legacy.

דְּבָרִים
D'varim, Words

THE PROFOUND TRANSFORMATION of Moses from a man hesitant to speak to the greatest prophet of Israel is evident with one word, *d'varim*. *D'varim*—'words'—can also mean 'things,' and it is the Hebrew name of the fifth and final book of the Torah. *D'varim* contains Moses's three great discourses to the people before his death, including his farewell song.

Deuteronomy, the English name of the book, is from the Greek *Deuteronomion* and the Latin *Deuteronomium*, meaning 'second law.' In the form of three sermons, Deuteronomy is a recap of the journey of Israelites, as well as laws and instructions previously given to the future nation, while introducing new laws and giving the people the charge to be faithful to God. The oldest name for the book is *Mishneh Torah*, or Repetition of the Torah, deriving from the commandment that the king is commanded to write a copy of the Torah and to study it daily (Deuteronomy 17:18).

D'varim is the plural of *davar*, meaning 'speech, discourse, saying, word, report, utterance, or command,' as in 'God's command.' The French ArtScroll *Chumash* translates *d'varim* as '*paroles*,' which can be translated as 'words' but can also mean 'song lyrics' or 'speech.' This is consistent with the Tosefta's view that in the opening of Deuteronomy, *d'varim* refers to both the written words of Torah and the spoken words of the Oral Law.

The Ten Commandments are called the *Aseret HaD'varim*, alternatively translated as the 'Ten Words' or 'Ten Utterances' (Exodus 34:28). Moses reminds the people that when God spoke to them out of the fire, they heard "the sound of words" (Deuteronomy 4:12).

Moses's valedictory addresses of Deuteronomy come from the man who initially demurs from God's calling. In his first encounter with God at the Burning Bush, Moses says, "I am not a man of words" (Exodus 4:10), not a man of *d'varim*, which, in the end, becomes the name of his book of words. By the end of his life, this man with no words becomes the great orator of Israel.

No Words

Today I have no words
For You, God.
None.
Yesterday,
The day before,
And the day before that,
I had words,
So many words,
Thousands of words
To share with You.
Perhaps tomorrow
There will be more.
Today I have no words
For You, God.
None.

Be with me
In my breathing,
In the quiet
That fills the space
Between us.
Be with me.
Give me the words
I need to hear.
Give me the words
I need to say.

Today I have no words
For You, God.
Do You have words
For me?

חֲזָק
Chazak, Strong

WHEN MOSES charges Joshua with leading the people into the Promised Land, he blesses Joshua with the words *chazak ve-ematz*, sometimes translated as 'be strong and of good courage' (Soncino), alternatively as 'be strong and resolute' (Plaut). According to Klein, the roots of the two words—*chet-zayin-kof* and *alef-mem-tzadi*—are synonyms meaning 'to be strong,' with the latter holding the additional element of 'to be bold.' The word *ometz* means 'strength, might, courage, boldness.'

Moses uses this combination three times to install Joshua into office, once in private (Deuteronomy 31:6) and twice in front of the people (31:7, 23). The Talmud (*Sanhedrin* 8a) notices a difference between the two public charges: "you shall go with this people into the land" versus "you shall bring the Israelites into the land." The Sages say this reflects two forms of leadership: collaborative and autocratic.

The charge *chazak ve-ematz* is repeated by God twice in the first chapter of the Book of Joshua. First, Joshua is told to be "strong and resolute" in apportioning the land to the tribes (Joshua 1:6). Immediately after, God instructs Joshua to be "very strong and resolute in order to observe faithfully the Torah" (1:7).

B'reishit Rabbah 6 understands this verse to mean that Joshua was reading from a Torah scroll at the very moment when God said, "*Chazak*." Based on this midrash, in Ashkenazic communities at the conclusion of each book of Torah in Shabbat worship, the congregation stands and calls out, "*Chazak, chazak, v'nit-chazeik*," an expression with the implied blessing that "we should go from strength to strength." Then the Torah reader repeats that phrase. In some Sephardic congregations, it is the custom to say, "*Chazak uvaruch*," which is short for *chazak uvaruch t'hiyhe* (be strong and blessed), at the conclusion of every *aliyah* to the Torah.

Twelve times the Torah tells us that God freed the Israelites from bondage *b'yad chazakah*, 'with a strong hand.' Five of those instances say both 'a strong hand and an outstretched arm.' The Talmud (*B'rachot* 32b) teaches that four things require strength: Torah, good deeds, prayer, and worldly occupations.

Be Strong and Be Blessed

My courage is in my heartbeat
And my open arms,
In my wisdom and my pulsing veins,
In trusting my vision and speaking my truth.
Chazak ve-ematz.
Be strong and of good courage.

My power is in surrender
To the unknown,
In traveling the long road out
And finding the long road home,
In my embrace of joyous adventure.
Chazak uvaruch.
Be strong and be blessed.

My majesty is in my deeds
My word and my mission,
In a breath of crisp morning air
And the shimmering sky at twilight,
Robes of humility and service.
Chazak, chazak, v'nit-chazeik.
Be strong, be strong, and we will be strong.

Journeys

❃

וַיֹּאמֶר יהוה אֶל־אַבְרָם לֶךְ־לְךָ מֵאַרְצְךָ וּמִמּוֹלַדְתְּךָ
וּמִבֵּית אָבִיךָ אֶל־הָאָרֶץ אֲשֶׁר אַרְאֶךָּ.

The Eternal One said to Abram,
"Go forth from your land, your birthplace,
your father's house, to the land that I will show you.
—Genesis 12:1

FROM THE MOMENT Abraham set out from Ur Kasdim on a journey
to what would become the Promised Land, we have been a wandering people. We go, we return, and we have dreams along the way.
These words are about the journeys of our ancestors—including *lech*
(go), *shuv* (return), and *teivah* (ark)—as well as their encounters along
the way, with the words *sulam* (ladder), *anan* (cloud), and Sinai. Two
of the words are also names of books of the Torah, *Sh'mot* (Exodus;
'names') and *B'midbar* (Numbers; 'in wilderness'). Notably absent
from this list is the word for journey itself, *nasa*, which is discussed in
this book's acknowledgments.

To us, the Talmud (*B'rachot* 29b) offers this advice, directly from
Elijah the Prophet: "Do not get angry and you will not sin. Do not
get drunk and you will not sin. And when you set out on a journey,
consult with your Creator, then set out." And how are we instructed
in that same passage of Talmud to consult with God? By saying *t'filat
haderech*, the traveler's prayer, as we set off on our way.

לֶךְ
Lech, Go

LECH IS THE IMPERATIVE form of the verb *halach*, meaning 'to walk, to go.' To embrace its power and full implication, put an exclamation point after it: "Go!" *Lech* is perhaps best known in the two-word phrase *lech l'cha*—'go forth'—with which God sends Abram off on a journey of discovery (Genesis 12:1).

Forms of *halach*—with its varied understandings—are common throughout *Tanach*. The root *hei-lamed-chaf* can mean 'go, proceed, move, walk, go away, depart, to cause to depart, lead, guide.' It can be used with animals, geography, or inanimate objects. The Torah uses this verb to explain that the Tigris River 'flows' east (Genesis 2:14). It's used when the floodwaters lift Noah's ark, and depending on the translation, it 'went,' 'drifted,' or 'coursed' upon the waters (7:18). Used figuratively, *halach* is a contranym, a word containing its own contradiction: it can mean 'to live' or 'to die.'

The Rabbis compare the use of this verb with both Noah's and Abraham's relationship with God. The Torah states that *et haElohim hit-halech Noach*, "Noah walked with God" (Genesis 6:9). Contrast this with God's command to Abraham: *Hit-haleich l'fanai*, "Walk before Me" (17:1). Noah walked with God by doing God's will. According to the Talmud (*Yoma* 28b), Abraham walked before God to prepare the world for Torah by practicing all of God's laws even before the Torah was written. This is the proof text: "Abraham hearkened to My voice and kept My charge, My commands, My statutes, and My laws" (26:5).

The imperative *lech* appears in several poetic combinations with other one-syllable imperatives: *kach valeich*, 'take and go' (Genesis 12:19, 24:51); *lech reid*, 'go down' (Exodus 19:24, 32:7); and *kum leich*, 'get up, go' (Genesis 28:2; Deuteronomy 10:11). Twice Jonah is told to *kum leich* (Jonah 1:2, 3:2). The phrase *lech l'cha* is perhaps the most enigmatic (Genesis 12:1). Colloquially, we might translate it as 'get up and go!' Alternatively, it can be rendered interpretively as 'go for yourself,' 'go with yourself,' 'go to yourself,' and 'go by yourself.' Each reflects a different aspect of a journey of discovery.

Go

Go for yourself.
Go with yourself.
Go to yourself.
Go by yourself.
But always, always,
Walk in the direction of God.
Walk in the direction of adventure.
Walk in the direction of prayer, joy, and wonder,
The direction of questions and mysteries,
The landscape of eternity,
The horizon of your heart.

שוב

Shuv, Return

AFTER ABRAHAM CHARGES his servant Eliezer with finding a wife for Isaac, Eliezer asks a question that seems straightforward at first, but is in fact a bit odd (Genesis 24:5). If the mission fails, he asks, shall he "*return* your son back to the land *you* came from?" But how, Chizkuni asks in his commentary, can Isaac return to a place he has never been?

Shin-vav-bet—the root of *shuv*, 'to return, turn back, come again, go again'—is also the root of *t'shuvah*, 'repentance.' The meaning 'repentance,' however, is a postbiblical usage. In the Torah, *shuv* typically holds the literal meaning of physical return: of a person to a place (Exodus 13:17; Numbers 14:3), of a person to another person (Genesis 16:9, 22:5), of a thing to its place (Genesis 8:3; Exodus 14:26), or of property to its original owner (Leviticus 25:10, 13).

When the angels visit Abraham and Sarah announcing the future birth of their child, the text uses a doubled form of the verb, *shov ashuv* (Genesis 18:10). A doubled verb is typically understood as emphatic. According to Rashi, the angel is saying that, in a year's time, God will return to the couple, and Sarah will have a son. Ramban compares this use with the meaning of *shav* in Deuteronomy 30:3, in which God promises the return of the nation to the land after a future exile.

The evolution of *t'shuvah* to mean 'repentance' is hinted at when Moses asked God to *shuv*, to return from anger and renounce punishment of the people after the incident of the Golden Calf (Exodus 32:12). It is suggested again when Eliezer uses another doubled form of the verb—*hehasheiv ashiv*—to ask if he should take Isaac to Abraham's homeland if the mission to find Isaac a wife fails (Genesis 24:5), raising Chizkuni's question. Rabbi Reuven Chaim Klein responds that even though Isaac has never been to his father's homeland, it was considered Isaac's "natural place," the place of his roots, the place from which his righteous nature emerged. The physical location is symbolic of his essence. *T'shuvah*, then, is the return to righteousness, which is one's natural spiritual state of being.

Barriers

There is no barrier—
No gate, no fence, no blockade—
That can keep you
Away from God,
That can bar your return
To your natural human state
Of righteousness and dignity,
Save the barriers
You place in your own way.

Return home
To yourself
Even if you've never been there,
Even if you've never met you,
Even if you feel like a stranger
To yourself.

סֻלָּם
Sulam, Ladder

IN ALL OF *TANACH*, there is only one *sulam*, only one ladder, Jacob's ladder. Like a dream, the word shows up and then disappears. "He dreamed, and lo—a ladder was set on the ground, with its top reaching to heaven, and lo—angels of God going up and coming down on it" (Genesis 28:12).

Sulam, a hapax legomenon—a word that appears only once in all of *Tanach*—means 'ladder, stairway, highway.' The root, which is uncertain, may come from *samach-lamed-lamed*, meaning 'to cast up a highway.' In Jacob's dream, it is a highway cast up to the sky, a stairway to the heavens.

There is an allusion to prophecy in this dream. *B'reishit Rabbah* 68:12–14 notes that the *g'matria* for *sulam* is 130, the same as the word *Sinai*, hinting that Torah would be given at Sinai. There are also hints of spiritual instruction. Levi Yitzchak of Berditchev says that Jacob's vision represents human beings who, though standing on earth, focus on the heavens. Or HaChayim says that the ladder is the mystical aspect of the human soul. Sforno on Genesis 28:17 says that it signifies the place that prayers ascend to heaven.

In fanciful fashion, the Rabbis of the Talmud (*Chulin* 91b) try to calculate the width of the ladder. In the story of the dream, the words for going up and coming down—*olim v'yordim*—are both plural. As a result, the Rabbis deduce that in the dream, two angels are ascending the *sulam* and two are descending it simultaneously. Thus, the ladder had to be wide enough for four angels. Using a quote from the Book of Daniel, and creative midrashic interpretation, the Rabbis deduce that the ladder was eight thousand parasangs wide, or thirty-two thousand miles. A ladder wide enough for four angels is a highway wide enough for all of humanity to reach heaven and earth.

Wooden Ladder

When I was a child
I imagined a great marble staircase
From heaven to earth.
A gleaming avenue
With polished balustrades
And an arched entrance in the sky,
Emerging directly from God's holy abode,
Full of light radiating from scores of angels
Visiting earth and returning to heaven.

Now I wonder
If the ladder wasn't made
Of simple wooden planks,
Subject to wind and rain,
Subject to the perils of misuse
The decay of neglect,
And failures of maintenance.
Perhaps it got so rickety
That it fell to the earth
And is now gathering dust
In some yet to be rediscovered *genizah*,
Waiting to be repaired.

שְׁמוֹת
Sh'mot, Names

SH'MOT, THE HEBREW NAME of the second book of Torah—corresponding to the English Exodus—means 'names.' It is the plural of *shem*, 'name.' Exodus begins with a recap of the names of those who entered Egypt, a repetition of the list found in Genesis 46:8–27. Rashi says that the names are repeated to show how dear these individuals were to God, that God remembers them by name.

In its various uses, *shem* can mean 'name, designation, reputation, renown, fame.' *HaShem*, 'the Name,' is used by many as a respectful surrogate for any of God's revealed names when not in prayer or study. About half of the uses of the word *sh'mot* in Torah introduce lineages.

Calling the book about the journey out of Egypt "Names" might seem odd. The Hebrew title stems from the ancient convention of deriving titles from the first significant word of the text, unrelated to the primary content of the book. Rabbi Michael Hattin points out the role of names in Exodus. There are those whose names appear and disappear, like the midwives Shiphrah and Puah. There are individuals whose names are never given, like the daughter of Pharaoh or Pharaoh himself. Moses's parents and sister are unnamed at the beginning of the story. We learn his parents' names only when the clans are named (Exodus 6:14–25). Miriam's name is revealed when she takes the women to dance at the sea (15:20–21).

Sh'mot is also a book of names for God, notes Rabbi Jonathan Sacks. Here we learn God's name *Ehyeh*, 'I will be' (Exodus 3:14). We are told that God appeared to the patriarchs as *El Shaddai* (6:3). In the Decalogue, God makes it the first commandment to know that *Adonai Elohecha*—the Eternal your God—is the One who brought you out of slavery (20:2). God also reveals deeper meanings of the name *Adonai* in what has come to be known as the thirteen attributes of mercy (34:6–7).

As a book of names for God, and as a book of named and unnamed persons, *Sh'mot* may be a more appropriate title than it first appears.

Divine Names

Every word of Torah
Is a divine name,
A gateway to understanding,
A pathway to connection,
A doorway to being
With God.

Every word of Torah
Is your name,
An invitation to yearn,
A summons to surrender,
A calling to be
With God.

God, who knows your name,
Remembers you,
And holds you dear,
Even when your journey
Leads to *mitzrayim*,
The narrow place.
Even on the journey into exile,
The path is toward redemption.

You have been given God's names,
As a gift for your wanderings,
To bring *Adonai* with you,
And to hold *Elohim* dear,
Even when your journey
Leads to *mitzrayim*,
The narrow place.
Even on the journey into exile,
The path is toward redemption.

תֵּבָה
Teivah, Ark

LIKE A BOAT DISAPPEARING over the horizon, the word *teivah*, 'ark,' shows up early in Genesis and then is gone, making only a brief reappearance in Exodus. After that, the disappearance is complete, not only from Torah, but from all of *Tanach*.

Teivah—meaning 'ark' or 'box'—is the name for two remarkably different water vessels: Noah's ark and the basket that carries baby Moses on the Nile. A *teivah* is rudderless, without sails or oars, guided by the will and the hand of God, requiring faith and surrender. It's a central feature of the Flood story, mentioned twenty-six times. Used only twice in Moses's story, the *teivah* is literally a plot vehicle, carrying him briefly in the river.

Compare the two crafts. Noah builds his vessel and leads everyone aboard; Moses is put into the vessel, built for him by his mother. Noah's craft must carry him on the raging waters for a year; it is his home. Moses floats on the river; it is his cradle. While Noah's *teivah* is crowded with people and animals, Moses is the sole occupant.

In its two biblical uses, a *teivah* is used to convey living beings. Klein notes that *teivah* is likely an Egyptian loanword meaning 'box' or 'coffin.' Together, the shape of the Hebrew letters—תבה—form a rectangle, like a coffin. There's irony here. God's prophet, heralding God's dominion over Pharaoh and all earthly kings, emerges from an Egyptian coffin.

The meaning and use of *teivah* has evolved since biblical times. The Rabbis of the Mishnah understood it to mean 'word,' and its usage expanded to overlap with the word *aron*—'ark, closet'—as in the ark for holding *sifrei Torah* or, in Sephardic communities, the bimah.

The Mussar work *Kav HaYashar—The Just Measure*—employs the *malei*, or full spelling of the word, *tav-yod-bet-hei*, to create a word scramble. Rewriting the order of the letters yields *bayit HaShem*, 'the house of God.' From this it concludes that *Shechinah*, the female indwelling presence of God, is called an ark, a *teivah*.

Two Arks

Noah was a salty dog,
An old seaman
Who built his boat
To ride the waves
Of God's wrath.

Moses was a future prince,
A baby
Sent on a journey
To become a prophet
And redeemer of his people.

An ark can be a giant vessel
That carries all of life,
Or a tiny basket
To carry one soul.
But an ark,
Without oar or rudder,
Always moves
By God's hand.

Let the vessels of redemption
Carry us across rough seas,
And bring prophets of God
To walk in our midst.

סִינַי
Sinai, Sinai

THE MOUNTAIN OF REVELATION, the mountain upon which God gives Moses the Ten Commandments, is the spiritual heart of the Sinai wilderness. The word *Sinai* typically appears in the Torah with one of two modifiers, either *midbar*, 'wilderness,' or *har*, 'mount.' In the collective Jewish conscious, however, when we say "Sinai," we do not think of the desert wilderness; we think of the mountain from which God gave Torah.

Sinai has another name. Mount Horeb is called "the mountain of God" (Exodus 3:1). The Rabbis consider Horeb and Sinai to be names for the same place. When he arrives at Horeb, Moses encounters God through a burning bush (Exodus 3:2). The Hebrew used for bush, *s'neh*, is spelled with a *samech* and a *nun*, like Sinai. According to *Pirkei D'Rabbi Eliezer* 41, "From the day when the heavens and the earth were created, the name of the mountain was Horeb. When the Holy One was revealed unto Moses out of the thornbush, because of the word for the thornbush, it was called Sinai."

The location of Mount Sinai is a mystery. The common belief is that the Sinai of Torah is a mountain called Jabel Musa in the southern Sinai. There is no archaeological evidence in the Sinai peninsula, however, of any encampments or mass wanderings of people, and none, in particular, around Jabel Musa. One recently debated theory is that the real Mount Sinai is Mount Karkom in the Negev, in part because of the presence of artifacts, although the theory has few proponents. Another theory, based on the description of Mount Sinai as trembling, with fire and smoke (Exodus 19:18), is that Sinai was a volcano, possibly placing it in northwest Saudi Arabia. This theory has also been generally dismissed. Mount Sinai was perhaps a volcano of a different variety.

The Volcano

Sinai was a volcano of Torah,
Explosions of wisdom and love,
The fire of God's word pouring forth,
Thunder in the air,
Tremors in the ground,
Sending a plume of holy ash
High into the sky,
Fine ash, now invisible,
Still settling slowly on the earth,
Ash that speaks,
Bringing new wisdom,
New insights,
New beauty,
As it arrives
From the heavens
In every generation.

עָנָן
Anan, Cloud

ON THE DAY that the *Mishkan*—the Tabernacle, the Tent of Meeting—was completed, a cloud descended and rested upon it (Exodus 40:34). Whenever the cloud rested, the Children of Israel camped; when it lifted, the people would break camp and journey on (Numbers 9:21). A cloud rested on Mount Sinai when the Ten Commandments were given (Exodus 24:15).

Clouds serve as physical and spiritual compasses for the newly freed Hebrew slaves and the emerging Israelite nation. The midrash (*B'reishit Rabbah* 56:1) says that a cloud pointed Abraham to the place on Mount Moriah where he was to sacrifice his son, Isaac. Throughout Sarah's life, a cloud hovered above the entrance to her tent. When Sarah died, the cloud departed, but when Rebekah came, the cloud returned, along with other blessings, including a candle that would burn from one Shabbat to the next (*B'reishit Rabbah* 60:16).

The simple meaning of *anan* is 'cloud, cloud-mass,' and it can also mean 'thunder cloud' or 'rainbow cloud.' The symbol of God's covenant after the Flood is a rainbow appearing in the clouds.

Other midrashim say that God wrapped Moses in a cloud to protect him from the angels, who were jealous of him; that a cloud of divine glory appeared at Aaron's death, gradually covering him until he disappeared; that Moses was sanctified by the cloud to receive the Torah on Sinai; and that when Moses's life was ending, a cloud of glory surrounded Joshua, his successor.

"I made the Israelite people live in booths when I brought them out of the land of Egypt" (Leviticus 23:43). Both Rashi and Rambam understand these booths as 'clouds of glory' that protected the wandering people.

As to the pillar of cloud, Rabbi Noa Kushner notes in *The Torah: A Women's Commentary* that "the cloud does not blanket and obscure, as we expect clouds to do; instead, it is contained in a pillar and provides direction for the Israelites." Here, the natural behavior of clouds is bent toward God's purpose and God's will.

A Cloud of Glory

Imagine seeing
A cloud
Like this . . .
Alive
Luminous
Radiant
Contained
In a pillar
That doesn't
Shift or change
Or drift away.
A cloud of glory
Hiding God within,
A compass leading
To a Promised Land.

Imagine a cloud
Of the Divine Presence—
Shechinah—
Dwelling above your tent,
Blessing your bread,
Keeping your lantern lit.

Imagine a cloud
Of glory
Holding you close and dear,
Keeping you safe,
Surrounding you
As you wander,
So safe you can hear
The Divine Word
In awe and wonder.

בְּמִדְבַּר
B'midbar, In Wilderness

THE ISRAELITES PASS through many wildernesses on the journey to Torah, to nationhood, and from Egypt to the Promised Land: the wilderness of Zin, the wilderness of Moab, and, of course, the Sinai wilderness.

B'midbar is the Hebrew name of the Torah's fourth book, Numbers, commonly translated as 'in the wilderness.' That's because the word is part of a noun pair, *b'midbar Sinai*, 'in the wilderness of Sinai.' Looking at just *b'midbar* in isolation, without the noun pair or definite article, Rabbi Steven Kushner provides the interpretive definition 'in wilderness.' The foundation of the word is *midbar*, according to Klein originally meaning 'pasturage,' literally 'the place whither cattle are driven.' Moses first encounters God at Mount Horeb after driving his father-in-law's flock into the *midbar* (Exodus 3:1), a foreshadowing of Revelation at Sinai.

Midbar is also translated as 'desert,' but the English connotation of a barren landscape hostile to life doesn't capture the Hebrew. According to the JPS commentary, *midbar* is "a region of uninhabited and unirrigated pastureland." Moses drives the flock into the desert-wilderness to pasture.

The Rabbis say that one can only acquire Torah wisdom 'in wilderness.' According to *B'midbar Rabbah* 1:7, "Anyone who does not make themselves ownerless like the wilderness cannot acquire the wisdom and the Torah." By emptying oneself of preconceptions, by allowing for deep spiritual experience, by becoming open to the possibility of encountering hidden treasures in a seemingly barren landscape, one becomes ready to find Torah.

If different vowels are used with the *dalet-bet-reish* root, the four letters of *midbar* yields *m'dabeir*, meaning 'speaker' or 'speaking.' In the wilderness, God speaks. In the wilderness, we can hear God.

O You Hills, O You Sands

Speak to me,
O you hills!
Did my father pass this way?
Did my mother draw water
From some secret well?
Did I dream of angels and blessings?
Did I dream of God's voice
In the stillness and the silent surrender?

Speak to me,
O you sands!
What ancient beauty have you captured?
What silent yearning springs up
To water my heart?
What wisdom still flows
From your depths?
What secret treasures
Do you hold dear?

Let me know the music of your valleys.
Let me hear the heartbeat
Beneath your thousand stones.
Let me remember
The ancient promise of home.

Speak to me
From the place where
Sand and hill and sky meet
In perfect silence,
In perfect wisdom,
In perfect love.

Peoplehood

כִּי עַם קָדוֹשׁ אַתָּה לַיהוה אֱלֹהֶיךָ בְּךָ בָּחַר יהוה אֱלֹהֶיךָ
לִהְיוֹת לוֹ לְעַם סְגֻלָּה מִכֹּל הָעַמִּים אֲשֶׁר עַל־פְּנֵי הָאֲדָמָה.

For you are a people consecrated to the Eternal your God:
of all the peoples on earth the Eternal your God chose you
to be God's treasured people.
—Deuteronomy 7:6

THIS PASSAGE appears nearly word-for-word twice in the Torah,
the second time in Deuteronomy 14:2. These are the only two times
the Israelites are called both *am kadosh*, 'a holy people,' and *am s'gulah*, 'a treasured people,' in the same passage. Peoplehood for the
freed Hebrew slaves is the destination of Torah, which we'll explore
with these words: *am* (people), *Yisrael* (Israel), *Ivri* (Hebrew), *ger*
(stranger), and *b'rit* (covenant). *Chesed* (loving-kindness) is included
in this section because of its association with the word *b'rit*.

The midrash (*Sifrei D'varim* 343) relates that all the other nations
of the world were offered Torah before the Israelites. Each asked,
"What is written in it?" and each found a reason to reject the gift.
Only the Israelites said, "All that the Eternal has spoken we will faithfully do!" (Exodus 24:7), sometimes translated, "We will do and we
will listen." The Israelites committed to living the Torah before actually hearing its contents. In this way, the people chose God. When the
people said that "we will do and we will listen," the Talmud relates, a
divine voice announced from the heavens, "Who revealed to My children this secret that the ministering angels use?" (*Shabbat* 88a).

עַם

Am, People

ON THE DAY they accepted Torah upon themselves, and all the generations to come, the Israelites became "the people of the Eternal your God" (Deuteronomy 27:9). Accepting the covenant was the ultimate transformational act for the former slaves. The common bond of Torah solidified peoplehood.

Am—'people, nation'—is spelled *ayin-mem* and can also mean 'kinsman, relative.' There is a strong common lineage of this word in Semitic and pre-Semitic languages, with Klein listing nine related words. According to Klein, all these words probably meant 'those united' or 'those related.' The Hebrew derives from the base *ayin-mem-mem*, meaning 'to join, connect.' The connecting preposition *im*, 'with,' is also spelled *ayin-mem*. While there are other words for 'nation' in *Tanach*, *am* is by far the most common, appearing three times as often as *goy*.

The first use of *am* comes in the story of the Tower of Babel, about a people with a common language who try to build a tower to reach heaven. According to Rashi, they had common customs. According to Ibn Ezra, they had a common religion. According to Radak, they were of one mind. God thwarts their efforts to achieve a common goal by confounding their language, thereby creating different peoples. Contrast this with what God does for the Israelites, giving the people a common religion, common customs, and common goals as the way to forge a nation.

Three times the Israelites are called an *am s'gulah*. *S'gulah* means 'possession, treasure.' The concept of a treasured people is first introduced when God tells the people that if they fulfill the covenant, they will be to God *li s'gulah mikol haamim*, "My treasured possession among all the peoples" (Exodus 19:5). Five times the people are called *am kadosh*, 'a holy nation.' Taken together, *am s'gulah* and *am kadosh* confer the status of 'a holy people, treasured by God.'

A Treasured People

You,
Holy One,
Call us Your *am s'gulah*,
Your treasured people,
Your treasured possession,
A people You hold dear.

When will we see each other
As a treasure?
These Jews, rejecting those Jews;
Those Jews, rejecting other Jews.
When will we see each other
As a holy people?

You,
Holy One,
Call us Your *am kadosh*,
Your holy people,
Holy in our acceptance
And in living Your Torah.

God of Old,
Guide us back to each other
With reverence and understanding.
Renew our days with love.
Then we will build
A temple of song to Your holy name,
Resounding from heart to heart,
From soul to soul,
From generation to generation,
The whole people of Israel.

יִשְׂרָאֵל
Yisrael, Israel

AFTER A LONG NIGHT wrestling with an angel, Jacob is told that his name will be changed to *Yisrael*, 'Israel' (Genesis 32:29). Several chapters later, God confers that new name upon him (Genesis 35:10).

Yisrael is a theophoric name combining *yisra* and *El*, a name for God previously examined in this volume. The root of *yisra* is *sin-reish-hei*—meaning 'to fight, strive, contend'—resulting in the meaning 'he contends with God.' Borrowing from the story, the phrase "God wrestlers" has become a contemporary self-definition of the Jewish people. The result of combining *yisra* and *El*, however, is ambiguous.

In a *Haaretz* article, Elon Gilad notes that "the verb in theophoric names in the ancient Near East, and in ancient Israel in particular, should describe an attribute of the deity, not of the person." So, based on that rule, *yisra* probably described the god *El*, not the people. In *The Torah: A Women's Commentary*, Dr. Tamara Cohn Eskenazi writes that "the original meaning of this two-part name cannot be stated definitively. In most cases, *El* is a noun meaning 'God,' but sometimes it has a more general sense of 'divine' or 'superlative.' Also unclear is whether *El* is subject or object of the name's verbal portion, which itself is ambiguous. Thus this name can be construed as 'he struggles with God,' or 'God struggles,' or 'God rules,' or 'his struggle is mighty,' and more."

The meaning 'God rules' stems from the possible relationship between our root *sin-reish-hei* and another root, *sin-reish-reish*, meaning 'he ruled, reigned, dominated.' Ramban says the first part of *Yisrael* comes from a third root, *yod-shin-reish*, meaing 'straight, right, pleasing.' In *Mei HaShiloach*, Rabbi Mordechai Leiner says that this yields 'straight ahead, God' but might also mean 'straight to God.'

Even after the new name is conferred upon him, the text continues to use both names for Jacob—*Yaakov* and *Yisrael*. Rabbi Benno Jacob says that each particular usage of Jacob's two names has a purpose. Our patriarch is Jacob when his material and physical aspects are dominant and Israel when his spiritual side prevails.

Return to Me

O Israel,
My people,
Fly your heart
Straight to God,
Like an arrow of love,
Flying to the heavens.

Aren't you tired
Of wrestling with My angels,
Of wrestling with your life,
Of wrestling with Me?
Aren't you tired
Of the struggle with your nature,
Of the struggle with your heart,
Of the struggle with Me?

O Israel,
My people,
Give yourself a new name
And return to Me,
Like an arrow of love,
Flying to the heavens
With hope and joy,
Straight and true.
Flying to the heavens,
Flying home.

עִבְרִי
Ivri, Hebrew

IN THE WAR of the four kings against the five, Abram is referred to as *ha-ivri*, 'the Hebrew' (Genesis 14:13). It's startling in its matter-of-fact usage. The word appears for the first time as if readers would already know that Abraham—then named Abram—is a Hebrew and what that means.

Befitting the collection of wandering peoples led by Abram, the word *ivri*—Hebrew—is of unknown and debated origins. According to some scholars, it is rooted in the proper name Eber, Abraham's ancestor. Midrash says that when Noah divided up the world among his three sons, the Land of Israel fell to the portion of Shem—*eretz ha-ivri-im*, 'the land of the Hebrews'—named after Shem's most prominent offspring, Eber.

According to other scholars, *ivri* is formed from a Semitic root meaning 'beyond, other side, across.' This would most likely render *ivri* as meaning 'from the other side' of the Euphrates. Geographically, Abraham came from the other side of the river.

Most scholars agree that *ivri* is somehow connected to the Akkadian *hapiru* or *habiru*, derived from a root that meant 'passersby,' connecting it to the Hebrew *ayin-bet-reish*, 'to pass.' The Akkadian *hapiru* is also connected to a word meaning 'dust, clay,' adding a derogatory element. Rather than identifying a particular people, it may have been used to designate a social class uprooted by ethnic upheavals and forced to migrate; thus it would be a term of social status. It might be from *apiru*, 'stateless people.' It appears in text as an exonym (non-native term) for the inhabitants of the Land of Israel.

Our Sages say that Eber, Noah's great-great-grandson, lived on a higher spiritual plane than most of the world, as did Abraham. This interpretation blends the genealogical sense of the word with the idea of something beyond this world, envisioning Abraham crossing over from a different plane of spirituality.

The Other Side

We came
From the other side
Of the river,
From some other nation,
Some other home,
Crossing borders
And oceans
And dreams,
Wandering toward God.

We came
From the other side
Of history,
From an ancient past,
And a heavenly future,
Seeing the world
When the One God
Unites all nations
And all peoples
With love.

We come
From the other side
Of eternity,
To dwell in the place where
The finite and the infinite meet,
The place where
The holiness and the mundane dance,
The place where
Now and forever laugh at such simple ideas
Of the Divine.

גֵּר
Ger, Stranger

NO LESS THAN THIRTY-SIX times, the Torah tells us not to oppress the stranger. Both Rashi and Ibn Ezra explain succinctly: the stranger—along with the widow and the orphan—is powerless. God further extends the simple admonitions against oppressing the stranger: strangers are given equal protection under the law (Leviticus 19:34).

The root of *ger*—'foreigner, stranger, temporary dweller, newcomer'—is *gimel-vav-reish*, meaning 'to sojourn, dwell.' The root, Klein notes, likely meant 'to turn off, leave the way.' The stranger has 'turned off' from the journey, to dwell in a foreign land. A *ger* was a resident alien who was a free person but without political rights, generally someone from another land. While negotiating for Sarah's burial place in a field near Hebron, Abraham calls himself a *ger toshav*, a 'resident alien' (Genesis 23:4).

Ibn Ezra notes a relationship between *ger* and the word *gargir*, 'berry.' He says that a stranger who is resident in another land "is like a berry plucked from a branch." Rabbeinu Bachya embellishes the idea, saying that a stranger is like "an isolated berry at the far end of a solitary branch." Having been strangers in Egypt, Torah explains, "you know the feelings of the stranger" (Exodus 23:9). Moses echoes this sentiment by naming his son Gershom, explaining, "I have been a stranger in a foreign land" (Exodus 2:22).

"Cursed be the one who subverts the rights of the stranger, the fatherless, and the widow" (Deuteronomy 27:19). Perhaps more startling than this curse—or the admonitions that the law must apply equally to the *ger* and the citizen (Leviticus 19:34; Numbers 15:15–16)—is that we are commanded to love the stranger (Deuteronomy 10:19).

In Rabbinic times, *ger* took on the meaning of 'convert.' The Rabbis derive the principle of complete acceptance of the convert from the Torah's attitude toward the *ger*. Rabbi Hanan Schlesinger says that the idea of *ger* as convert is hinted in the Torah when it distinguishes between a stranger residing with the Israelites who has taken on some of the customs of the people, and a *ger*, who is simply passing through.

Estranged

There are always
Strangers among us,
Some, so obvious,
Some, so hidden,
Estranged inside their hearts
By the circumstances of life,
By strange workings of the mind,
And unusual workings of the body.
Estranged
Inside the gates,
Living perilously,
Like a berry at the end of the branch,
Resident but alien,
Never fully embraced.

Once, my father's father's grandfather,
In ancient days,
Bought a cave
In a field near Hebron,
So, at least, our family
Could become
Fully resident
In death.

בְּרִית
B'rit, Covenant

JUDAISM IS A COVENANTAL FAITH. We are bound to God and to each other by that pact, enshrined in Torah and lived through the laws, customs, and traditions of this people.

The word *b'rit*—'covenant, treaty, alliance'—is possibly derived from a *bet-reish-tav* root, meaning 'to eat bread.' In ancient times, Klein explains, it was customary for those concluding a treaty or alliance to partake of a meal. Another possibility comes from a second root of the same letters meaning 'to choose.' The parties to a covenant or alliance choose to enter that relationship. Although a minority view among scholars, Ibn Eza and the Baal HaTurim hold this view.

Ramban dervies the word *b'rit* from *bara*, 'created.' Rabbeinu Bachya explains that *b'rit*, spelled *bet-reish-yod-tav*, represents the first two and last two letters of *b'reisheit*, 'in beginning.' God, from the very start, establishes a covenant of the continuity of human life with the righteous of the world. This covenant is exemplified with Noah being saved from the flood that destroyed the world and is enshrined in the appearance of a rainbow in the clouds after a storm.

Ibn Ezra notes that some rabbis hold that *b'rit* means a 'cut boundary.' The root letters *bet-reish-tav* can be rearranged to *bet-tav-reish*, meaning 'to cut off.' This midrashic idea connects the common current usage of the word *b'rit*—as a short form of *b'rit milah*—to the term 'circumcision.' In Torah *b'rit* is not a word for the act of circumcision, as it is today; rather the act of circumcision, *milah*, is a form of literally embodying the *b'rit*, embodying the covenant. Another act of covenantal embodiment is keeping the Sabbath, which is called a *b'rit olam*, 'a covenant for eternity.'

Creation begins and ends with covenant, as does all of Torah. God asserts to the people that the covenant is not only with the assembled masses—from the highest office holder to the common worker—but also with future generations (Deuteronomy 29:13–14). This eternal covenant binds us all.

Promises

My great-uncle Samuel,
His mother Chaiyke,
Her father Mashe,
And every generation
From here back to Sinai,
From here back to Mount Gerizim and Mount Ebal,
From here back to the border of the Promised Land,
Were bound by the pledge
Of our ancestors,
A pledge made for all of us,
To live lives of Torah and mitzvot.

Each generation of this people
Somehow,
At times joyously,
At times in spite of ourselves,
Nonetheless chooses to reaffirm the pact
Made on our behalf,
Made in an ancient time,
In the wilderness
Between what was
And what might be.

חֶסֶד
Chesed, Loving-Kindness

CHESED—'kindness, goodness, mercy'—comes from the root *chet-samech-dalet*, meaning 'to be kind, to be pious.' *Chesed* is a contranym: it can mean both 'to be kind' and 'to be ashamed,' although the former meaning dominates in *Tanach*.

Chesed is one of God's thirteen attributes of mercy (Exodus 34:6–7), which we recite as part of the Yom Kippur liturgy. In this context *chesed* follows *rav*, 'abundance'—God's abundant kindness. Sforno says that this means God is inclined toward leniency in administering justice. Dr. Jeremy Benstein notes that *chesed* is a culturally laden word that's difficult to translate. It does not map onto just one English-language value concept. Rather, it is rendered variously as 'grace, faithfulness, kindness,' and also 'loving-kindness, charity, favor, goodness, benevolence.'

A remarkable juxtaposition of words can be found the last time *chesed* is used in the Torah, when it is twice paired with *b'rit*, 'covenant.' The phrases are *habrit v'hachesed* (Deuteronomy 7:9) and *et habrit v'et hachesed* (7:12). The translations vary but fall into two broad categories: those that link *b'rit* and *chesed* as one phrase—that is, God keeps the 'covenant faithfully'—and those that show them as separate concepts—that is, God keeps both 'the covenant and the kindness.' Rabbi Jonathan Sacks notes, "Covenant is essentially reciprocal. Two people or entities pledge themselves to one another, each committing to a responsibility. . . . *Chesed*, in contrast, has no if/then quality; it is given out of the goodness of the giver, regardless of the worth of the recipient."

Our relationship with God, it seems, is both conditional and unconditional. God's pledge is both to keep the covenant—the details of the mutual commitments enshrined in Torah—and, no matter what, to sustain the flow of divine love.

Claim God's Love

When the Children of Israel
Assemble before You
In holy convocation,
We assert the covenant,
The promise You made
To our ancestors.
We claim the right
To Your kindness
And unconditional love.
The covenant that binds
And the love that endures.

When the Children of Israel
Assemble together
In holy convocation,
We assert our love,
The promise we made
To You in the wilderness.
We affirm the responsibility
To live Your Torah
And to teach its ways.
The covenant that binds
And the love that endures.

Mitzvot

כִּי הַמִּצְוָה הַזֹּאת אֲשֶׁר אָנֹכִי מְצַוְּךָ הַיּוֹם
לֹא־נִפְלֵאת הִוא מִמְּךָ וְלֹא רְחֹקָה הִוא.

Surely, this Instruction which I enjoin upon you this day
is not too baffling for you, nor is it beyond reach.
—Deuteronomy 30:11

THE WORD *MITZVAH*, singular of *mitzvot*, means 'command, commandment, precept' but is often translated as 'instruction.' It's from the root *tzadi-vav-hei*, meaning 'to command, order.' Although we commonly use the word today to mean 'good deed,' its meaning in the Torah is both prescriptive and proscriptive: the things we must and must not do. Mitzvot establish our relationship with God. The first three words in this section describe our relationship with the Divine in broad strokes: *Torah*, *sh'ma* (hear), and *v'ahavta* (and you shall love). Two words in this chapter represent the mysterious mitzvot: *t'cheilet* (sky blue) and *t'ruah* (loud blast). We continue with a word that might have easily fit into the chapter on Creation, *tov* (good). It, too, can be seen as a word that describes our relationship with God. We close with *chataah* (sin), that which gets in the way of a relationship with the Divine.

The Talmud (*Kiddushin* 39b) relates that those who perform one mitzvah have goodness bestowed them, their lives are lengthened, and they inherit life in the world-to-come. Also from the Talmud (*Makot* 25b), we learn that the reward extends not only to persons performing the mitzvah, but to those who facilitate the performance of mitzvot by others.

תּוֹרָה
Torah, Teaching

ACCORDING TO THE TALMUD, before God created the universe, God created Torah, one of the seven things brought into being before Creation (*P'sachim* 54a). Perhaps God needed to create Torah as a precursor to creating the world. *B'reishit Rabbah* 1:1 makes the bold claim that God used Torah as the blueprint for all of Creation.

Torah is defined as 'instruction, law, teaching, doctrine, direction.' The word is derived from the root *yod-reish-hei*, meaning 'to teach, instruct.' Some scholars connect the root to an Aramaic word meaning 'he taught,' others to the Arabic 'he handed down,' and others to the Akkadian 'to guide.' The same root has a second meaning, 'to throw, cast, or shoot.' Combining the meanings of the two roots, we might say that Torah is the straight teaching. Rabbi Lawrence Kushner defines Torah as 'the way.'

Rav Samson Raphael Hirsch derives *torah* from an alternative root, *hei-reish-hei*, meaning 'to conceive.' He writes, "Just as an embryo grows from a seed that is implanted at conception, so too God's teachings plant a seed, so to speak, which develops in the recipient to an ever-greater consciousness of good."

Like an author writing a memoir, the Torah is unabashedly unafraid to talk about itself. The Torah tells us that it is our inheritance (Deuteronomy 33:4). It asks us: "What other nation has a teaching as perfect as this?" (Deuteronomy 4:8). "Cursed be whoever will not uphold the terms of this Teaching and observe them.—And all the people shall say, Amen." (Deuteronomy 27:26).

In all, the word *torah* appears in the Five Books of Moses fifty-six times, twenty-two of them in Deuteronomy, the great recapitulation of God's miracles and God's laws. Three of Maimonides's Thirteen Principles of Faith speak of the Torah: belief in the primacy of Torah, Moses's prophecy; belief in the divine origin of the Torah; and belief in the immutability of the Torah. Together, that would make Torah God's autobiography.

Autobiography

My Torah,
My autobiography
Is, in truth,
The story
Of you.

What joy you inspire in heaven
When you grapple with My words,
When you confront the contrasts
And the dissonances . . .
Love and war,
Anger and mercy,
Creation and destruction,
Heroes and villains,
Artists and zealots,
Laws that make sense,
Laws that make no sense,
To you.

My Torah,
My autobiography
Is, in truth,
The story
Of us.

שְׁמַע
Sh'ma, Hear

HEAR. LISTEN. OBEY. Understand. Pay attention! The word *sh'ma* is a wake-up call. Hearken to God, to Torah, to the mitzvot, to the unity and singularity of God's name.

Klein defines the root *shin-mem-ayin* as 'hear,' with similar words found in multiple Semitic and proto-Hebraic languages. Although it is a verb, in modern parlance it is most commonly thought of as a proper noun, the name of a central rubric of Jewish prayer. Sometimes *sh'ma* refers to the six Hebrew words of Deuteronomy 6:4, usually translated as "Hear, O Israel! The Eternal is our God, the Eternal alone." Sometimes it refers to the paragraph (Deuteronomy 6:4–9); sometimes to the three paragraphs of Torah central to the rubric (Deuteronomy 6:4–9, 11:13–21; Numbers 15:37–41); and sometimes to the entire rubric of prayer, including the *Bar'chu* and the prayers before and after the Torah passages, or the *Sh'ma* and Its Blessings. It is always about the centrality of faith in God as a pillar of Judaism.

In the Torah scroll—and in printed texts of the prayer, such as mezuzot and *t'fillin*—the last letter of the word, the *ayin*, is larger than the rest of the word. One interpretation is that a potential misspelling of the Hebrew, with an *alef* in the place of the *ayin*, would yield a homophone meaning 'perhaps,' changing the connotation of the verse from the declarative to an interrogative—yielding "Perhaps, O Israel . . ."— and casting doubt on the declaration that God is One.

Sh'ma is also the opening word of the *Sh'ma Koleinu*, the sixteenth benediction of the weekday *Amidah*, a longer version of which is part of the High Holy Day liturgy. We ask God to hear our prayers, to hear our voices, and to hear our deepest yearnings. Just having been told to listen to God in the recitation of the *Sh'ma*—to hear God's laws, mitzvot, and instructions—we then pray for God to hear our prayers.

The Sound of Hearing

Let me hear
The whisper of You,
Where faith meets doubt,
Where speaking surrenders to listening,
Where You are everything.

Holy One,
Hear the sound of my hearing,
A quiet yearning as my heart bends
To You.
And make my prayers
One with Yours.

וְאָהַבְתָּ
V'ahavta, And You Shall Love

GOD COMMANDS US TO LOVE. How strange! Four times in Torah, the wandering Hebrew nation is told, "And you shall love [*v'ahavta*]"— functionally an imperative, even though grammatically a future verb, according to Dr. Joel Hoffman. Twice the command is to love God, including the paragraph known from the *Sh'ma* by that same name (Deuteronomy 6:5–9). Twice in Leviticus we are commanded to love others: our neighbors (19:18) and the stranger (19:34).

The instruction to love God appears more often in the form *l'ahavah*, 'to love.' The core of both words is *ahavah*. Its root, *alef-hei-bet*, means 'love' or 'like.' It describes the love of particular things, of human-to-human love, of love from human to God, and of God's love for humanity. It can mean self-love, romantic love, or sexual desire. It can refer to God's love of a specific individual or of the people of Israel as a whole.

Some examples: In Genesis, the word can refer to parental love, as Abraham for Isaac (22:2) and Rebekah for Jacob (25:28). It depicts Isaac's feelings for Rebekah (24:67), Isaac's love of meat (27:4), and Leah's yearning to be loved by Jacob (29:32). As a noun, *ahavah* occurs only once in all of Torah. God brought the people out of Egypt with a mighty hand *ki mei-ahavat Adonai et-chem*, "because of the Eternal's love for you" (Deuteronomy 7:8).

The Sages debate whether loving God can be commanded. Their classic response is that we show our love of God by doing the mitzvot. Barbara Binder Kadden writes that our prayer book offers a more contemporary response. Before reciting the *Sh'ma*, we are reminded of God's love for us, in the morning with the prayer *Ahavah Rabbah*, and in the evening with *Ahavat Olam*. She writes, "In both prayers we are reminded first of God's deep love for the people of Israel. This declaration of God's love is then made tangible through the gift of Torah and mitzvot. We respond to *Ahavah Rabbah* and *Ahavat Olam* with the *Sh'ma*, declaring that *Adonai* is our God and *Adonai* is One. It is only then that we are commanded to 'love God with all of your heart, all of your soul, and with all of your might.'" God seeks a reciprocal relationship.

Heart, Soul, Might

When you choose
וְאָהַבְתָּ (*v'ahavta*) to love
אֵת יהוה אֱלֹהֶיךָ (*et Adonai Elohecha*) Adonai your God
בְּכָל־לְבָבְךָ (*b'chol l'vavcha*) with all your heart,
You must choose to love yourself
The way God already does.

When you choose
וְאָהַבְתָּ (*v'ahavta*) to love
אֵת יהוה אֱלֹהֶיךָ (*et Adonai Elohecha*) Adonai your God
בְּכָל־נַפְשְׁךָ (*b'chol nafsh'cha*) with all your soul,
You must choose to love others
The way God already does.

When you choose
וְאָהַבְתָּ (*v'ahavta*) to love
אֵת יהוה אֱלֹהֶיךָ (*et Adonai Elohecha*) Adonai your God
בְּכָל־מְאֹדֶךָ (*b'chol m'odecha*) with all your might,
You must choose to love Creation
The way God already does.

When you choose to love everything and everyone
The way God already does,
You will flow with grace through the river of life
To the Soul of the universe.

לְמַעַן תִּזְכְּרוּ וַעֲשִׂיתֶם אֶת־כָּל־מִצְוֹתָי וִהְיִיתֶם קְדֹשִׁים לֵאלֹהֵיכֶם.
L'maan tizk'ru vaasitem et kol mitzvotai
Vih'yitem k'doshim l'Eloheichem.
Be mindful of my mitzvot and do them,
And you will become holy unto your God.

תְּכֵלֶת
T'cheilet, Sky Blue

T'CHEILET IS A BLUISH COLOR, translated in various texts alternatively as 'blue,' 'blue-green,' 'sky blue,' 'violet blue,' and 'turquoise blue.' It's one of the colors used in the fabric for the curtain of the Tabernacle (Exodus 26:1). In this way, *t'cheilet* connects us to God by connecting us to the very structure of God's house on earth. It's also the color of a single dyed fringe originally part of the tzitzit, the fringes of the tallit (Numbers 15:37), a practice once lost and then recently revived after the rediscovery of the process to create the dye. These ritual fringes are meant to remind us of the mitzvot. *T'cheilet*, a color used for both fringes and curtains, connects us to both service to God and God's chosen place in the world.

The Talmud (*B'rachot* 9b) uses the contrast between white fringes and blue fringes as a sort of clothing-based clock to determine the time for reciting the morning *Sh'ma*. The *Sh'ma* can be recited in the morning once a person can distinguish between the *t'cheilet* and white fringes on a tallit, although Rabbi Eliezer dissents, opining that the *Sh'ma* can be said when one can distinguish between sky blue and leek green. The *Zohar* associates white with the divine attribute of mercy, and *t'cheilet* with justice, comparing *t'cheilet* to the inside of a flame (*Zohar, Sh'lach L'cha* 175). *Sefer HaChinuch* identifies white with the physical and *t'cheilet* with the spiritual.

Rabbi Meir is quoted in the Talmud (*M'nachot* 43b) as saying, "What is different about *t'cheilet* from all other types of colors such that it was chosen for the mitzvah of ritual fringes? It is because *t'cheilet* is similar in its color to the sea, and the sea is similar to the sky, and the sky is similar to the Throne of Glory." And so, the sea and the sky might also be thought of as visible reminders of our relationship with God.

Hallelujah of Color

Weave the color of the sky
Into the fabric of your days,
The fabric of your life,
The threads that bind your days
To the holiness of living.

Weave the color of the sea
Into the song of your heart,
The music of your longings,
The tide that binds your nights
To the chorus of the sky.

Weave the color of prayer
Into the voice of your soul,
The song of your yearnings,
The notes that bind your heart
To the wonder of Creation.

Let me walk with the radiance of heaven.
Let me sing with the echo of eternity.
Let me pray with the pulse of being.
Let me become a sky blue,
Purple, violet, turquoise, crimson,
Lavender, lupine, sapphire, topaz
Illumination of blessings,
A hallelujah of color
Doing God's will,
Lifting praises to the throne of glory,
Declaring that God is One.

תְּרוּעָה
T'ruah, Loud Blast

ROSH HASHANAH is called *zichron t'ruah mikra kodesh*, "a sacred occasion commemorated with loud blasts" (Leviticus 23:24). From this verse, it's unclear if the Torah is telling us to mark Rosh HaShanah by blowing a shofar or by blowing the *chatzotz'rot*, the silver trumpets used to stir the Israelites into action. Translations of *t'ruah* vary across Torah commentaries, including 'sounding,' 'loud blasts,' 'blast of horns,' and 'shofar blasts.'

Klein defines *t'ruah* as 'shout, cry, alarm,' as well as 'a succession of tremulous notes of the shofar or trumpet.' There are two related roots: *reish-vav-ayin*, meaning 'shout, to give a blast (with a horn or trumpet),' and *tav-reish-ayin*, 'to blow a horn or trumpet, to warn, to sound an alarm.'

The Torah offers no direct reference to specifically blowing the shofar on Rosh HaShanah, instead using *t'ruah* as a general term for sounding a horn. In contrast, the word *shofar* is specifically used for the sounding of horns on Yom Kippur to announce the Jubilee Year (Leviticus 25:8–10). This ambiguity is compounded by the use of the *t'ruah* in other Torah passages in conjunction with blowing the *chatzotz'rot*. Rabbinic logic resolved the matter by determining that the intent of using the word *t'ruah* is that the shofar should be sounded on Rosh HaShanah.

That left another question: What is the sound of *t'ruah*? The Rabbis never doubted that the shofar note called *t'kiah* was sounded as one long blast. But the Talmud (*Rosh HaShanah* 33b) considers three possibilities for how to sound a *t'ruah*:

- Three short, straight blasts, what we now call *sh'varim*
- Nine staccato blasts—*t'ruah*
- A combination of both—*sh'varim-t'ruah*

Unable to come to a definitive answer, in classic Rabbinic fashion, the debate is resolved by determining that all three possible forms of the *t'ruah* blast would be sounded on Rosh HaShanah.

The Sound of Holiness

When God, in creating,
Began to create,
Silence hovered over the face of the deep.
And God said,
T'kiah. T'ruah. T'kiah.

Holiness has a sound.
Part swoosh of blood in the veins,
Part hum from the edge of the universe,
Part stillness, part vibration,
Part life entering a newborn,
Part life leaving the deceased,
Part dissonance, part resonance,
A sound that can only be heard
With the heart.

When God, in creating,
Began to create,
God spoke in music,
Giving us the shofar
As a vessel to hold the divine voice,
And as an instrument
To summon awe and wonder,
So we might become,
In our own lives
And in the world,
T'kiah g'dolah.

טוֹב
Tov, Good

GOOD IS EVERYWHERE—the word, anyway. *Tov*, 'good,' in any form—noun, verb, adjective, place—is used nearly 650 times in *Tanach*. All but four books of the Bible have at least one use of the word. It is overwhelmingly used as an adjective, 565 times. *Tov* can mean 'good, pleasant, agreeable, kind, well, a good thing, welfare.' The root, *tet-vav-bet*, means 'to be good, to be pleasing.'

The first seven uses of *tov* in the Torah are found in the Creation story in the first chapter of Genesis. This raises the question: What does it mean for something to be "good" when "bad" didn't yet exist? The Soncino *Chumash* notes that in the context of Creation, "it was good" means that Creation served the will of the Creator. At the end of Creation, "it was very good," *tov m'od* (Genesis 1:31), means that all of Creation perfectly served God's will.

The first use of *lo tov*, 'not good,' also occurs in Genesis, when God says that it is not good for the human to be alone (Genesis 2:18). Rav Mike Feuer considers this line a hint as to why God created the universe and humanity, in particular. Perhaps in this passage God is talking about Godself; it is *lo tov* for God to be alone.

Good is not a subjective judgment: it is not relative to bad. Rather, *tov* is a state of being, the state of fulfilling the will of the Creator. Perhaps that's what changed after Adam and Eve ate fruit from the Tree of Knowledge of Good and Evil: they were no longer fulfilling the will of their Maker. This interpretation of the word also casts light on the final use of *tov* in the Torah: "See, I set before you this day life and good, and death and evil" (Deuteronomy 30:15). The path of life is in fulfilling God's will.

The Good Path

The good path
Is God's path,
Given through Torah,
Lived through mitzvot,
Fostered by tradition,
Sustained by teaching,
Enlivened with love,
Enlarged by community,
Resonant with song,
Resounding with joy,
Punctuated with fears,
Striving, ever striving,
To fulfill
The will
Of our Maker.

חֲטָאָה
Chataah, Sin

TORAH GIVES US THREE WORDS for 'sin': *avon*, *fesha*, and *chataah*. They appear together when God passes by Moses on Sinai reciting the thirteen attributes of divine mercy (Exodus 34:7). The specific meanings and differences between these three words are debated by the Rabbis, but none of them are used to describe the actions of Adam, Eve, or the snake. The first term for sin to appear in Torah is *chatat*. After Abel's offering is accepted and Cain's rejected, Cain's "face fell" (Genesis 4:5). God says to Cain, "Would you not do well to lift it? For if you do not do well—sin is a demon at the door; you are the one it craves, and yet you can govern it" (Genesis 4:7).

Used as a noun, *chataah* is a contranym: it can mean either 'sin' or 'sin offering'—the action of sinning and the action atoning for sin. The root of *chataah* is *chet-tet-alef*, meaning to 'miss the mark, to go wrong, to sin.'

The Talmud (*Yoma* 36b) explains that *cheit* refers to inadvertent sins, *avon* to intentional sins, and *pesha* (the word has a *fei* when preceded by a *vav* and a *pei* otherwise) to sins of rebellion. Ever since then, the Rabbis have wrestled with the definitions and the differences. Malbim explains that the words reflect motive: a *cheit* occurs when one is swayed by physical temptations; an *avon* is when one's intellect has been negatively persuaded; and a *pesha* refers to committing sins shamelessly as a way of rebelling against God. Rabbi Shlomo Pappenheim of Breslau writes that *chet* is a lack of mindfulness when sinning; *avon* is the sin of one who thinks too much; and *pesha* refers to the sin of somebody who knows that the act is forbidden and completely wrong.

Finding modern language to describe sin is equally challenging. In creating the *machzor Mishkan HaNefesh*, Rabbis Janet Marder and Shelly Marder note the broad use of language for sin in the volume, including the following: evil, wickedness, depravity, crimes, brute power, malevolence, guilt, shame, failings, offense, brokenness, immorality, destructiveness, malice, wrongs, treachery, transgressions, mistakes, cruelty, stumbled, fallen, failure, harm, misdeeds, errors, defiant acts, and inner darkness.

Sin Crouches

Sin crouches at my door,
The door to my home,
And the door to my heart.

Yet I must venture out,
Beyond the gates and boundaries,
To encounter the world.
Where else can we do God's will?
Where else can we build and heal?

Sin crouches at the gates,
Waiting, always waiting,
For a wounded soul.

Offerings

꙰

קְחוּ מֵאִתְּכֶם תְּרוּמָה לַיהוה כֹּל נְדִיב לִבּוֹ יְבִיאֶהָ אֵת תְּרוּמַת יהוה.

Take from among you gifts to the Eternal;
everyone whose heart is so moved shall bring them.
—Exodus 35:5

After God tells Moses to ask the people for precious gifts to use in constructing the Tabernacle—gold, silver, fabrics, jewels, spices among them—the people are overcome with generosity. They bring so much material that the artisans tell Moses that they have more than is needed, and Moses tells the people to stop (Exodus 36:5–7). Offerings in Torah are both freewill and mandatory. We begin the third book of the Torah with a surprising word in the context of offerings: *vayikra*, '[God] called,' the Hebrew name for the Book of Leviticus. We'll examine the word in the light of being called into the service of God. We continue with the *Mishkan*, the Tabernacle, which is built with gifts and is also the place where gifts will be brought to God in the desert wanderings. Not surprising, we round out our examination of offerings with *bikurim* (first fruits), *korbanot* (sacrifices), *t'rumah* (offering), and *maaseir* (tithe). *Tamid* (always) concludes the list, both as the name of the twice daily sacrifices and in reference to other Temple rites.

In *Pirkei Avot* 5:8 we are told that when some people give tithes and others do not, "a famine from drought comes; some go hungry, and others are satisfied." When no one tithes, "a famine from tumult and drought comes." Commenting on this mishnah, Rabbeinu Yonah says that when those who fail to tithe go hungry, it is poetic justice. That is to say, we get the society that we create. Human or divine, when people fail to share their blessings, there are fewer blessings in the world.

וַיִּקְרָא
Vayikra, [God] Called

VAYIKRA—[GOD] CALLED—is the name of the Torah's great book of Levitical law, the Hebrew name for Leviticus. The root is *kof-reish-alef*, meaning to 'call, invoke, invite, name, proclaim, read aloud.'

The first use of *vayikra* comes when God calls the light "day" and in the same verse, with a different conjugation of the root, calls the darkness "night" (Genesis 1:5). Light had already been created two verses earlier. So what is happening here? Ramban holds that in this verse God is creating time. There seem to be two actions and two meanings implied by *vayikra* in this passage: the action of naming *and* the action of calling into being. Later, Adam names all the creatures (Genesis 2:20), but in this case *vayikra* has only one meaning. The human *vayikra* is different from the divine calling.

The divine *vayikra* has yet another aspect, which we find in the opening of Leviticus. The book begins, "The Eternal One called to Moses and spoke to him from the Tent of Meeting, saying" (1:1). This opening line has two verbs: *vayikra*, 'called,' and *vay'dabeir*, 'spoke.' God first called Moses; then God spoke to Moses. Rabbi Jonathan Sacks explains that *vayikra* was a summons, a calling to teach Torah to the people. Only after the summons came the words, *vay'dabeir*, which God spoke.

At the opening of Leviticus, the word *vayikra* contains a traditional scribal rarity. The last letter, an *alef*, is written smaller than its normal size. The Baal HaTurim says that Moses wanted to use the word *vayikar*, 'and it happened,' instead of *vayikra*. *Vayikar* is used in the story of the prophet Balaam, hired to curse the Hebrews (Numbers 23:4). Rashi says that *vayikar* implies that God appeared to Balaam only as a chance occurrence. Even though Moses wanted to use the more humble word *vayikar*, God told Moses to add the *alef*—*vayikra*—indicating that this was not a chance meeting, thus showing God's love for Moses. Because Moses was humble, he used a small *alef*.

God names. God calls into being. God summons.

God Called

Suddenly,
Without warning,
God called to the people, saying,
I gave words to Moses,
To entreat you,
To enlarge you,
To entrust to you.
They are yours now.

This is your calling,
and My question:
What choices will you make?
How will you live My Torah?
How will you teach My Torah?
How will you preserve and enlarge
My Torah in the world?

You have been offered a good path,
A path of life and love.
Torah is calling you.

Now, begin your own chapter,
With humility and love, thus:
"And God called out,
Summoning me,
Calling my life's mission into being . . ."

מִשְׁכָּן
Mishkan, Tabernacle

HOW CAN THE FINITE meet the Infinite? Where can humanity meet God? The Torah's answer: an in-between place, a place where God's glory can dwell on earth. For the desert wanderers, the place is the *Mishkan*, the Tabernacle constructed in the wilderness. The root of *mishkan*—'dwelling place, habitation, tabernacle'—is *shin-kaf-nun*, meaning to 'dwell, abide, nest.' *Mishkan* shares the same root as *Shechinah*, the feminine aspect of God. Tradition says that the feminine aspect of God resides on earth.

The Rabbis consider the words *Mishkan* and *Mikdash*, 'Sanctuary,' as interchangeable—the *Mishkan* being the elaborate yet portable version of God's Sanctuary. Indeed, the words are used as synonyms when God says, "Let them make Me a sanctuary that I may dwell among them" and immediately following when God instructs the exact pattern of the Tabernacle and its furnishings (Exodus 25:8–9).

Troubled by the idea that God wants or needs a physical place to dwell on earth, the Rabbis favor metaphoric interpretations. *B'midbar Rabbah* 12:13 compares the language of the creation of the universe in the first chapter of Genesis to the language used for the construction of the Tabernacle. The *Mishkan* is a universe in itself.

Saadyah Gaon speaks of three worlds: the terrestrial world, the *Mishkan*, and the human body, representing the macrocosm, intermediate world, and microcosm, respectively. Ibn Ezra takes that a step further, saying that God's glory fills the universe, *Shechinah* fills the *Mishkan*, and our divine souls fill our bodies. According to Rabbi Michael Hattin, these two commentators are asserting that we share a natural affinity with God, for the very makeup of our being somehow parallels God: "A cohesive connection between us and the Deity, though sometimes difficult to believe, is actually an innate feature of our own existence. Our soul longs for a profound bond with God."

Malbim wrote, "Each one of us needs to build God a Tabernacle in the recesses of our heart, by preparing ourselves to become a Sanctuary for God and a place for the dwelling of God's glory."

God Yearns

God yearns
For an invitation
To dwell among us.

So we create space
For God's arrival,
Opening our souls,
Opening our lives,
Building sanctuaries
For Torah and *t'filah*,
So *Shechinah* can appear
In the tabernacle of our hearts
With Her gifts of tenderness
And love.

We meet God
Somewhere between
A vision of heaven
And the reality of earth,
Yearning for God to stay present,
Yearning for God to dwell among us,
While God yearns
For an invitation
To dwell among us.

בִּכּוּרִים
Bikurim, First Fruits

A GIFT. A TITHE. A SACRIFICE. The distinction between these holy acts of giving by the Israelites can be lost on us, living thousands of years after our ancient agrarian ancestors and after service in the Temple ended. These offerings, brought to the Temple and given to the priestly class, each had its own purpose.

The Torah uses two words for 'first fruits' almost synonymously, *bikurim* and *reishit*. Although the connotation seems to be different, the action they represent—bringing first fruits as gift offerings to the Temple—is the same. Modern commentaries, regardless of which word is used in the Torah, generally refer to this act as *bikurim*.

The root of *bikurim*—*bet-kaf-reish*—means 'invested with birthright, firstborn.' This is the same root as *b'chor*, 'firstborn.' Based on the same general principle in Torah that the firstborn child and the firstborn animal belonged to God, the first fruits were to be brought to the Temple as gift offerings. Rashi, quoting *Mishnah Bikkurim* 1:3, says that this gift applied only to the "seven species" of agricultural products that bless the Land of Israel: wheat, barley, grapes, figs, pomegranates, olives, and dates. The connotation of *bikurim* appears to be chronological: literally, the first fruits that appear.

Reishit comes from the root *reish-alef-shin*, meaning 'head.' *Reishit* holds the meanings of 'beginning, first fruits, choicest parts.' It derives from the word *rosh*, meaning 'head, chief, leader, summit, beginning.' In all forms, *reishit* is used eighteen times in Torah, but only once with a *bet* prefix, forming the name of the first book of Torah, *B'reishit*. In the context of first fruits, the connotation of *reishit* appears to be qualitative: the very finest fruits of the year. When used together—in the form *reishit bikurei*, occurring only twice in the Torah (Exodus 23:19, 34:26)—translators typically render the meaning as 'choicest, first fruits.'

My First Fruits

Poetry
And song
Are the first fruits
Of my life,
The words I give back
To God as prayer.
Also my love for my children,
For you,
And life itself.

Only you know
The first fruits
Of your life.
The first and the finest
Of your thoughts and deeds.
Only you know
What you are willing
To offer the Eternal,
Creator of heaven and earth.

קָרְבָּנוֹת
Korbanot, Sacrifices

NEARLY ONE-FIFTH of Torah and one-third of Talmud deal with the ancient sacrificial practices known as *korbanot*—in the singular, *korban*, translated as 'offering, sacrifice, oblation.' This word for 'sacrifice' first appears in Leviticus, although sacrifices have been recorded throughout the Torah since Abel and Cain first made their fateful offerings to God (Genesis 4:3–4).

The root of *korban* is *kof-reish-bet*, meaning to 'come near, approach,' which is also the root of *hikriv*, 'approached, brought near.' In the first two books of Torah, *hikriv* means simply 'to approach,' (e.g., Genesis 12:11; Exodus 14:10). In the beginning of Leviticus, the word takes on a new meaning: 'offer a sacrifice' (1:2).

Rav Amnon Bazak notes that in Leviticus, God establishes a permanent location for the Divine to dwell on earth in the form of the Sanctuary. Then, and only then, could sacrifices be considered a way to come near to God. With a sanctuary there was a physical dimension to 'coming near,' and it was expressed, therefore, in a new use for the word *korban*.

In common English usage, "sacrifice" connotes giving up something of value for someone else's benefit. The ancients Israelites, however, did not think of their offerings in that way. Rather, the *korbanot* were an expression of love and the desire to draw near to God, much like a soon-to-be-treasured anniversary gift given to a beloved. Etymologically, "sacrifice" comes from the combination of *sacer* (sacred, holy) and *faciō* (do, make). The English word "sacrifice"—meaning 'to make holy'—is a profoundly different concept than the Hebrew *korban*, 'to draw near.'

Sacrifices were both communal and individual. The community offered two lambs each day—one in the morning and another in the afternoon—plus additional sacrifices on Shabbat, the holidays, and the new month. An individual was obligated to bring a sacrifice as atonement for sin and for ritual purity. Other individual sacrifices were voluntary, such as a thanksgiving offering. Mammals, birds, fruits, grains, and incense were all used as *korbanot*.

Draw Me Near

Draw me near to You
Ancient One,
God of my ancestors,
As I approach You
In my love and imperfection.

How I wish to be Your sanctuary,
The place where Your holiness dwells,
To live my life in service to Your will and Your word,
To become an offering
Of joy and song,
An offering
Of peace and repair.

Draw me near to You,
Rock and Shelter,
God of my people,
As I approach You
Seeking Your majesty
And Your blessing.

תְּרוּמָה
T'rumah, Offering

GOD SAYS TO MOSES, "Tell the Israelite people to bring Me gifts; you shall accept gifts for Me from every person whose heart is so moved" (Exodus 25:2). Meaning 'contribution, gift, offering,' *t'rumah* here refers to the voluntary gifts used to create the *Mishkan*, God's 'dwelling place' on earth (25:8). The usage of *t'rumah* then shifts to 'priestly dues from produce,' 'contribution to be set apart for priests,' and 'contribution for the Tabernacle.'

Later in that book, *t'rumah* takes on the additional meaning of 'elevation offering' (29:27), a separated portion of an offering ceremonially raised and lowered in dedication to God and afterward reserved for the officiating priest's use. Then, in the next chapter, when taking a census of military-aged men, the *t'rumah* is no longer voluntary; a half-shekel contribution is required per man (30:13).

Klein relates the word *t'rumah* to two roots, which highlight this evolution of the concept from 'voluntary donation' to 'required contribution.' The first, *reish-vav-mem*, means 'to be high, to be exalted, rise, to be haughty.' *T'rumah* is the verbal noun of *heirim*, 'he lifted up, he raised, he offered, he lifted up and presented.' The implication is that the gift—given in service to the divine will—gains an elevated status. Also by implication, the giver of gifts in service to God gains an elevated status.

The second root, *tav-resh-mem*, has the postbiblical Hebrew meaning 'to separate priestly dues, to contribute, to donate' to the Rabbis, thus strengthening the connection of the biblical usage to the idea of contributions set apart for the priests.

As we move through the Torah, the use of the word *t'rumah* gets tied up into the system of tithes. A different word is used specifically for 'freewill offering,' *n'davah*. In spite of becoming obligatory in the Rabbinic understanding of halachah, *t'rumah* never loses the tone and character of a gift.

Gifts of No Utility

Since the moment
We became aware
Of You,
We have been bringing gifts,
The best we have to offer.
Nothing of use
To You.
No, nothing of utility
In the realms of mystery
Beyond infinity and nothingness.
The meaning is in the giving,
In the offering,
In the action,
Full of gratitude and love,
In the bond forged
With offerings of the heart,
In the hope
That these gifts
Are received
With divine tenderness
And Eternal love.

מַעֲשֵׂר
Maaseir, Tithe

THE IDEA OF *MAASEIR*, the 'tithe' of 10 percent of certain produce, would seem to be straightforward. Yet the Torah's instructions are complicated—at times seemingly contradictory—and are tied into the offerings known as *t'rumot*. The early Rabbis harmonized these biblical instructions into a unified and codified set of laws and instructions. While the overall legal framework of *t'rumot* and *maasrot* is generally accepted by Rabbinic sources, the technical details of that system continue to be debated.

Maaseir is a noun that means 'tenth-part, tithe.' The root for *maaseir*, *ayin-sin-reish*, has two meanings. According to Klein, one is 'ten.' The original meaning was probably 'gathering, collection, union.' It is related to several Arabic words: *ashara*, 'he formed a community'; *ashira*, 'tribe'; and *ma'shar*, a group of ten men. Both the Hebrew and Arabic probably originally meant 'a group collection,' then became 'a group of ten,' and ultimately 'ten.' The other meaning for the root is 'to take the tenth part.'

The verb form of *maaseir*, rare in Torah, shows up twice in a row in Deuteronomy, in a form known as the infinitive absolute: *aseir t'aseir* (14:22). This type of repetition provides emphasis and in translation it typically adds 'you shall surely' to the verb—in this case, 'you shall surely tithe.' In the Talmud (*Shabbat* 119a), the Rabbis interpret this combination homiletically, substituting the word *titasheir*, 'to become wealthy,' for *t'aseir*. In doing so, they declare that the act of honest tithing increases wealth rather than decreasing it.

The rabbis also developed the concept of *maaseir k'safim*, 'tithing money,' which first appeared in rabbinic writings in Germany and France between the years 1200 and 1350. This substitute for biblical tithing is debated among the rabbis, both regarding whether it's an obligation, as well as how those funds can be used.

One-Tenth

How to measure
One-tenth of my heart?
One-tenth of my soul?
One-tenth of my might?

I tithe my joy to God,
An offering of gratitude and love.

How to measure
One-tenth of my grief?
One-tenth of my sorrow?
One-tenth of my despair?

I tithe my pain to God,
An offering of acceptance and surrender.

No,
Take it all.
Take all of my joy,
All of my grief,
As witness to my devotion to life,
However it may come,
Whatever it holds,
No matter what
Blessings or curses
You have labeled
With my name.

תָּמִיד
Tamid, Always

TAMID IS ALTERNATIVELY TRANSLATED as 'continuously, constantly, regularly, always, at all times.' Klein notes that the word might come from either of two roots. He favors *mem-vav-dalet* which is related to the Arabic *madda*, meaning 'he stretched, extended, prolonged, made to continue.' The other potential root, *mem-dalet-dalet*—meaning 'to measure'—is related to the Akkadian *madādu*, 'to measure the length of something.' Rabbi Howard Markose says that "to measure something from one end to the other is to continually take note of the size of the matter. So the *tamid* is that which is constantly under scrutiny." As a noun, it means 'continuity,' as in the continuity between generations.

In the Torah, *tamid* is most often used in connection with the Temple rites: *olat tamid*, the burnt offering brought twice daily; *eish tamid*, the fire burning perpetually on the altar; and *ner tamid*, the lamp lit every night that burned until morning.

In later books of the Bible, *tamid* is associated with Israel's devotion to God and God's steadfast love of Israel, which is how it often occurs in our prayer book—for example, from the weekday and Shabbat *Yotzeir*, "In Your goodness You daily renew creation"; and from the weekday *Amidah*, "And for all these things, O Sovereign, let Your name be forever praised and blessed."

Rabbi Chayim of Volozhin once asked his teacher, the Vilna Gaon, for a blessing. The master said, "May you always be worthy of two *tamid*s." Reb Chayim left happy, but the Vilna Gaon's students were confused—what did this mean? In the blessing, the Vilna Gaon invoked the two uses of the word *tamid* by Rabbi Moshe Isserles in *HaMapah*, his masterful commentary on the *Shulchan Aruch*. The book begins with the verse "I have set God always before me" (Psalm 16:8) and ends with "Contentment is a feast without end" (Proverbs 15:15). In this way, the Gaon blessed Reb Chayim to be humble before God, to be content in life, and to live in accordance with God's word.

Lamp, Eternal

Light my heart
Ablaze with Your love
And I will become
A lamp eternal
In service to Your holy name.

Let my soul
Be Your constant companion,
Humble and content,
Reliable and true,
A lantern to summon Your glory.

Let my life
Be a sign for the generations,
A beacon for the ages,
And I will live
In accordance with Your will.

Let my heart
Blaze with love for You,
So that all will see
That I have placed You before me,
Always and forever.

Holy Time

דַּבֵּר אֶל־בְּנֵי יִשְׂרָאֵל, וְאָמַרְתָּ אֲלֵהֶם, מוֹעֲדֵי יהוה,
אֲשֶׁר־תִּקְרְאוּ אֹתָם מִקְרָאֵי קֹדֶשׁ אֵלֶּה הֵם, מוֹעֲדָי.

Speak to the Israelite people and say to them:
These are My fixed times, the fixed times of the Eternal,
which you shall proclaim as sacred occasions.
—Leviticus 23:2

GOD SETS OUR SPIRITUAL CALENDAR, appointing the time and seasons of the Festivals and designating our weekly Sabbath. Holy time is central to Jewish life. Five separate Torah passages describe the holy days: Exodus 23:14–17; Exodus 34:18–23; Leviticus 23; Numbers 28–29; and Deuteronomy 16. If more evidence is needed to support the centrality of holy time, note that the first thing that God designates as holy is Shabbat (Genesis 2:3) and that the first command given to the entire nation is to mark the monthly new moons (Exodus 12:2). We begin our exploration of holy time with the foundational word *kadosh* (holy). We then examine the *sh'vi-i* (seventh), recognizing that our holy times often cycle in sevens or multiples of seven. Shabbat and many of the *mo-adim* (festivals), as well as the *Sh'mitah* (year of release) and the *Yoveil* (Jubilee year), are tied to the rhythm and the pattern of seven.

Along with the Torah, Shabbat is considered one of the most precious gifts that God gives the Jewish people. Commenting on Exodus 31:13, when God reiterates the commandment to "keep My sabbaths," the Talmud (*Shabbat* 10b) says that God also said to Moses, "I have a good gift in My treasure house. Shabbat is its name, and I seek to give it to Israel. Go inform them."

קָדוֹשׁ
Kadosh, Holy

THE SIMPLEST, YET IMPOSSIBLE, instruction in Torah is this: "You shall be holy, for I, the Eternal your God, am holy" (Leviticus 19:2). The verse is distinctive in that it provides a rationale for a commandment, writes Nachum Sarna. To have a close relationship with God, the people must emulate God. The 'you' is plural, as in 'you all' shall be holy.

The adjective *kadosh*, 'holy, sacred,' comes from the root *kof-dalet-shin*. In noun form, *kodesh*, it means 'holiness, sanctity.' The simple verb form, *kideish*, means 'was set apart, was consecrated, was forbidden.' The root has parallels in many languages in the Semitic family tree, including the Akkadian *quddushu*, 'to cleanse, to hallow, sanctify,' also meaning 'shining, pure.' Klein notes the original meaning of the root was likely 'to separate.'

The first use of the root as a verb appears as *vayikadeish*—God 'sanctifies' the seventh day (Genesis 2:3). Its first use as a noun is when God tells Moses to remove his sandals because the ground is *kodesh*, 'holy' (Exodus 3:5). Genesis introduces the concept of holy time, while Exodus introduces the concept of holy place. The root is used in Torah to describe Shabbat and the Festivals as *mikra-ei kodesh*, 'holy convocations.' It is embedded in the name of the inner sanctum of the Tabernacle, *Kodesh HaKodashim*, the Holy of Holies.

Many familiar terms stem from this root: *Kiddush*, the prayer over wine before the start of Shabbat and festivals; *Kaddish*, a prayer said in memory of the deceased; *K'dushah*, a portion of the *Amidah*; and *kiddushin*, the sanctification of a marriage. The *chevrah kadisha* is the Jewish burial society.

How can we humans hope to emulate God's holiness? According to Rashi, to be holy as God is holy means to refrain from forbidden sexual encounters. Ramban has a broader view: fulfilling all of Torah is the minimum criteria for emulating God's holiness. The true task, he says, is to exceed God's instructions.

You Shall Be Holy

You are
Standing on holy ground.
Your life is holy ground.

You are
Standing in the Holy of Holies.
Your life is the Holy of Holies.

You are
A shining and pure soul,
Sanctified into life by God.

Life is a holy convocation.
Holy time, holy place,
Holy image, holy space.

See holiness as the spark of the Divine,
Invisible to the naked eye,
The residue of God's presence,
The ripple of wonder
And the shiver of incomprehension
When the Infinite touches the finite
And the Divine touches the mundane.
And you shall be holy,
For God is holy.

שְׁבִיעִי
Sh'vi-i, Seventh

THE NUMBER SEVEN is woven into Torah and our lives. It first appears when we're told that on the seventh day—*yom hash'vi-i*—God completed the work of Creation and rested (Genesis 2:2). Seven represents divine completion.

Seven and seventh are straightforward words, *sheva* and *sh'vi-i*, both from the same root meaning seven, *shin-bet-ayin*. This prevalence of sevens in Torah and *Tanach* is profound. Dr. Elaine Goodfriend notes that sevens appear in our text in a variety of forms, including the number itself, in keywords that appear seven times, and in the story narrative.

Here's a sampling: Shabbat occurs every seven days, Shavuot comes seven weeks after Pesach begins, and both Pesach and Sukkot are seven days long. The *Sh'mitah* year occurs every seven years, and after seven cycles of Sh'mitah, the *Yoveil*, the Jubilee year, is declared. Boys are circumcised after seven days. The lampstand in the Tabernacle has seven lamps. The Levites kept watch at the entrance to the Tabernacle for seven days prior to its dedication.

Stories can simultaneously contain both obvious and subtle uses of the number seven. For example: Twice Jacob labors for Laban for seven years to marry Leah and Rachel (Genesis 29:20–30). In that story, the root *ayin-bet-dalet*, meaning 'work, labor,' occurs seven times. The repetition of roots often reinforces the content of the story. For example, in the story of Cain and Abel, the word *ach*, 'brother,' occurs seven times (Genesis 4). When Rebekah goes with Eliezer to marry Isaac, the narrative contains seven uses of the root *hei-lamed-chaf*, meaning 'to go' (Genesis 24).

Goodfriend writes, "Although the numbers one, two, and three occur more frequently, the number seven is the most important symbolic number in the Hebrew Bible. In many contexts, it conveys not just the number seven, but the idea of wholeness and perfection. As a result of the identification of the Israelite God with perfection, the number seven has also come to represent holiness."

Seven

There was evening,
And there was morning,
And God created seven.
It was quite natural,
The one coming after six.
The One who set numbers
Into motion
Couldn't help it.
Seven.
The perfection of it
Is the rhythm
Of all our journeys.
Seven.
The wholeness of it
Returns and returns
With blessings from beyond.

שַׁבָּת
Shabbat, Sabbath

THE SAGES SAY THAT SHABBAT, the Sabbath, is a taste of the world-to-come (Babylonian Talmud, *B'rachot* 57b). Whatever the "world-to-come" might have meant to the Sages, the general idea is clear enough: Shabbat is a bit of heaven that, once each week, comes to earth.

The root of the word *Shabbat*—'Sabbath, day of rest'—appears conjugated in Torah in both verb and noun forms, with a variety of meanings: 'week [the seven days from Sunday to Shabbat], feast, festival, years [meaning a period of seven years], Sabbatical year [*Sh'mitah*].' The root, *shin-bet-tav*, means 'to cease, desist, to rest.' The first uses of *Shabbat* in the Torah appear toward the beginning of Genesis (Genesis 2:1–3) and have become the preamble to reciting *Kiddush* on Friday night. After God completes Creation, God rests. Ironically, the root is conjugated here as a verb, *shavat*, an action word. The action of Shabbat is rest.

In the two sets of the Ten Commandments (Exodus 20; Deuteronomy 5), different verbs describe the obligation toward Shabbat: *shamor*, 'keep,' and *zachor*, 'remember,' parallel in requirement but with different actions. Rashbam says that remembering refers to past events. *Zachor* is to remember—in the sense of commemorate—the original Sabbath of God's cessation from creative activity. *Shamor* is to keep—in the sense of observe and guard—the Sabbath that arrives each week.

The Torah tells us explicitly the month and day of each festival, based on the arrival of the new moon, but how did we know the day of the week on which Shabbat would fall? Shabbat observance makes its appearance with the story of the manna. On the sixth day after the arrival of the first manna, God says, the next day would be Shabbat (Exodus 16:5). God picked the day, which we have observed ever since.

The phrase *Shabbat shabbaton* occurs six times in Torah (and once as *shabbaton Shabbat kodesh*), often translated as a noun-adjective combination, such as 'a Sabbath of complete rest.' Only Yom Kippur (Leviticus 16:31, 23:32), the *Sh'mitah* year (Leviticus 25:4), and Shabbat (Exodus 16:23, 31:15, 35:2; Leviticus 23:3) are called *Shabbat shabbaton*. *The Living Torah* renders the phrase with two nouns: 'a Sabbath of sabbaths.'

The Seventh Day

As the sixth day ends,
Anticipating the arrival of holiness and beauty,
The sun stands motionless,
The wind holds its breath,
The tides refrain,
And the earth shimmers
With its own ancient light,
Creation waits
With open arms,
Anticipating sweetness
And timeless gifts.

In the world-to-come,
When every day
Is Shabbat,
When every day
Is a day of complete rest,
When every day
Is a day of joy and song,
Will we still
Remember
That the seventh day
Is a gift?

Let me aspire,
Each week,
To a Shabbat
Of perfect rest,
Of perfect harmony,
Of perfect love
For God and life itself.

שְׁמִטָּה
Sh'mitah, Release

EVERY SEVEN YEARS the land is to be released from agricultural service, debts forgiven, and private fields made available for public gleaning. This is the *sh'nat haSh'mitah*, the 'year of release' (Deuteronomy 15:9). *Sh'mitah*, meaning 'omission of debts, remission, release'—is from the root *shin-mem-tet*, 'to let drop, to draw away, to slip off.'

Practicing *Sh'mitah* in a place where rain is scarce and famines long is a profound act of faith. The Torah is aware that the year of *Sh'mitah* exacts a toll, impacting three years of food supply. The harvest must be especially robust in the sixth year to provide that year's food and to support the lack of food in the seventh year and again in the eighth year, as a new grain harvest would only arrive roughly eight more months after planting. God says, "I will ordain My blessing for you in the sixth year, so that it shall yield a crop sufficient for three years" (Leviticus 25:21).

Although the word *Sh'mitah* first appears in Deuteronomy 15:1, the concept originates in Exodus 23:11, where it is called *sh'vi-it*—'seventh,' read in the context of the previous verse, 'seventh year.' In Leviticus it is described three ways: as a *Shabbat l'Adonai*, a 'Shabbat for God' (25:2); as a *Shabbat shabbaton*, a 'Sabbath of sabbaths' (25:14); and as a *Shabbat haaretz*, a 'Sabbath of the land' (25:6).

There is a paradox in releasing the land from agricultural service: the land continues to produce. According to Chizkuni, the land isn't tired; rather, as a Sabbath for God, *Sh'mitah* reminds us that the land belongs to its Maker. Rashi understands *Sh'mitah* as a Sabbath in honor of God's name. Sforno says that during this year the farmer, instead of "serving" the soil, spends a year serving God.

"What Sabbath does for the individual, *Sh'mitah* does for the nation," writes Rabbi Avraham Yitzchak HaKohen Kook, who highlights that *Sh'mitah* embeds communal generosity into Torah law. "On the *Sh'mitah*, our pure, inner spirit may be revealed as it truly is." Kook envisions a year "without tyrants or taskmaster . . . when a spirit of generosity rests on us all . . . a godly peace pervades all that breathes . . . and a holy spirit will be poured out upon all life."

Extravagant Generosity

The years
Pile on.
The weight
Of expectations
And dreams,
Of obligations
And commitments,
Can crush
Heart and soul.

Release yourself from toiling
And fussing
And fretting
For capital gain.
Let the land breathe
And your spirit soar
With extravagant generosity
And outrageous kindness.
Then, the earth will sigh,
Your eyes will shine,
A godly peace
Will rest in you,
And a spirit of holiness
Will pour forth
Throughout Creation.

יוֹבֵל
Yoveil, Jubilee

THE ENGLISH WORD "JUBILEE"—based on the Hebrew *Yoveil*—does not capture its biblical intent. *Yoveil* was to be proclaimed every forty-nine or fifty years (there is disagreement in Rabbinic discourse) with a blast of the shofar (Leviticus 25:9), the freeing of slaves, and the return of land holdings to their original owners and every person to their familial lands. Freedom and reunion. Society would get a twice-per-century reboot, although there is disagreement in Rabbinic discourse about whether the Jubilee took place in the forty-nineth or fiftieth year.

Yoveil is first used in the Torah as a term for shofar: "When the ram's horn [*yoveil*] sounds a long blast, they may go up on the mountain" (Exodus 19:13). *Yoveil* is the shofar blast announcing the Jubilee year. Klein defines *yoveil* as 'jubilee, year of jubilee,' as well as 'ram, ram's horn.' He says it was likely derived from the root *yod-bet-lamed*, meaning 'to bear, carry,' but originally meaning 'leader of the flock, bellwether.'

Ibn Ezra translates *yoveil* as 'sending away,' referring to releasing slaves. Ramban renders *yoveil* as 'liberty,' also referring to freeing slaves. He writes, "In my opinion, Scripture does not call the year *Yoveil* with reference to the blowing [of the shofar], but rather with reference to the liberty [that it brings]."

Netziv says that *yoveil* is an expression of moving from one place to another. "This is why the antelope is also referred to as a *yoveil*, because it is always moving from place to place." Chizkuni translates *yoveil* as 'to bring home,' which could refer to both the release of slaves and the return of familial lands. Ramban connects *yoveil* with the phrase *yivlei mayim* (Isaiah 30:25), meaning 'channels through which water is conveyed.' Building on this connection, Rabbeinu Bachya translates *yoveil* as 'rivulet'—a small stream of water—referring to the idea that during the *Yoveil*, everything flows back to its original source. Biblical scholar and translator Everett Fox renders *yoveil* as the 'year of homebringing.' The Torah is clear about this intent: "Each of you shall return to your holding and each of you shall return to your family" (Leviticus 25:10).

Release

So very few hear the call
To set free the slave within,
To release ourselves from
Judgment and sorrow.
So very few hear the call
To reclaim what is ours
And to return what is not.
To reunite with each other,
And to recover what has been lost.

How hard it is to forgive
The burdens of debt,
The commitments we took on
With hope and love,
To rediscover each other
With song and dance.

Let each day
Bring a taste of Jubilee,
To practice the art of following
The river,
Perhaps the one
That will lead us back,
Finally,
To a garden of delight.

מוֹעֵד
Mo-eid, Festival

ON THE FOURTH DAY of Creation, God made two great lights—the sun and the moon—to serve as signs of day, night, and the set times, known as *mo-adim*. The word is the plural of *mo-eid*, meaning 'appointed time, festival, appointed place, place of meeting, appointed sign, signal, festival sacrifice.' These definitions have the common theme of something being designated. The root is *yod-ayin-dalet*, 'to appoint.' God appoints sun and moon as signs to announce the festivals (Genesis 1:14–18).

The festivals are our regular, annual, communal appointments with God. Although they are ordained in multiple places in Torah, chapter 23 of Leviticus presents this list: Pesach, the Passover sacrifice; Chag HaMatzot, the Feast of Unleavened Bread; Reishit, time of first fruits; Shavuot, the Feast of Weeks; Yom T'ruah (Rosh HaShanah), the time of trumpets; Yom Kippur, the Day of Atonement; Sukkot, the Feast of Tabernacles; and Sh'mini Atzeret, the Eighth Day of Assembly. The list is bracketed by statements that these are the appointed seasons of God, taught by Moses (verses 4 and 44). Together, these two verses serve as the introduction to the festival morning *Kiddush*.

God speaks to Moses and Aaron from an appointed place. The text uses three terms for places to meet God: the *Ohel Mo-eid* (Tent of Meeting), the *Mishkan Ohel Mo-eid* (Tabernacle Tent of Meeting), and the *Mishkan* (Tabernacle). *Mishkan Ohel Mo-eid* and *Mishkan* refer to the same structure built in the center of the Hebrew encampment, but the *Ohel Mo-eid* appears to be a different structure.

After the incident of the Golden Calf, God decides not to personally lead the people, but rather to send an angel as guide (Exodus 32:34). God says, "I will not go in your midst" (33:3). Ibn Ezra interprets this second reference to mean that God would cancel plans to build the desert Tabernacle. There would be no place of meeting in the encampment. So Moses sets up his own Tent of Meeting outside of the camp (33:7–8)—an act of civil disobedience—and convinces God to relent. God leads the people as a pillar of cloud and as a pillar of fire, and the Tabernacle is built.

Reunion

Follow the moon and the stars
And you will always know
When to meet Me.
Our appointed times
And appointed seasons
Are set by signs in the sky.
When you look toward heaven,
And I look toward earth,
We will always know
When to find sacred reunion.

We have appointments
With each other,
You and Me,
That we must keep.

Mysteries

הַחַיִּים וְהַמָּוֶת נָתַתִּי לְפָנֶיךָ הַבְּרָכָה וְהַקְּלָלָה וּבָחַרְתָּ בַּחַיִּים.

I have put before you life and death, blessing and curse.
Choose life.
—Deuteronomy 30:19

OUR EXAMINATION OF MYSTERIES in the Torah extends from our examination of Creation, beginning with the word *tzohar* (light source), apparently a reference to the window at the top of Noah's ark but perhaps something more enigmatic. Six of the eight words in this section are paired contrasts: *Tzohar*, which brings holy light to the ark, is a unique antidote to the unholy *choshech* (darkness) of the ninth plague. *B'rachah* (blessing) and *arur* (cursed) are obvious contrasts. God tells us to choose between them. While *man* (manna) represents the longest running miracle that God gives the Israelites, *pesel* (idol) represents the ultimate rejection of God's love. We close with two additional mysteries: *R'fa* (heal) asks the question of whether healing is a human intervention contrary to God's will. *Amen* (truly) explores the mystical meaning of the word we use to end every blessing.

The Talmud (*B'rachot* 54a) asserts, "One recites a blessing for the bad just as for the good. For bad tidings, one recites a special blessing: *Baruch Dayan ha-emet*, 'Blessed is the true Judge.'" It goes on (60b–61b) to place before us two spiritual challenges: the first, to accept bad tidings with the same joy with which we accept good tidings; the second, said in the name of Rabbi Akiva: "One must always accustom oneself to say: 'Everything that God does, God does for the best.'"

צֹהַר
Tzohar, Light Source

AT THE TOP OF NOAH'S ARK, the Torah gives us an enigma, a mystery that has captured the imagination of rabbis for millennia. Noah is told to build the ark with a *tzohar* at the apex, which has been alternatively translated in Torah commentaries as 'window,' 'opening,' 'roof,' and 'skylight.' The unifying element in these translations is that the *tzohar* is a source of light for the ark. The word shares the same root as *tzohorayim*, 'noon'—*tzadi-hei-reish*—the time when the sun is highest in the sky.

Tzohar is a hapax legomenon (Genesis 6:16). Without other references in the text to help establish its meaning, the word leaves much to the imagination. Some rabbis say that when Noah "opened the window of the ark" (8:6)—the word used here being *chalon*, 'window'—it was the *tzohar* that he opened. Thus, *tzohar* could mean 'window.' Yet during the deluge, there would be no sun. What, then, was the source of the light?

In the Talmud (*Sanhedrin* 108a), Rabbi Yochanan says that God commanded Noah to "set precious stones and jewels in the ark so that they will shine for you as the afternoon sun." In the midrash (*B'reishit Rabbah* 31:11), Rabbi Levi says the *tzohar* is an opalescent gem. Rashi conceives of the *tzohar* as a luminous stone holding light from the first day of Creation, a ray of the secret light reserved for the righteous. From here, midrashic interpretation becomes fanciful, weaving a variety of legends identifying the *tzohar* as a jewel containing a remnant of primordial light, which God gave to Adam and Eve, and subsequently to be passed through the generations to—among others—Noah, Abraham, Joseph, and Moses.

According to Klein, some scholars connect the root of *tzohar* to another root, *zayin-hei-reish*, which means 'to shine,' the root for the name of the primary book of Kabbalah, the *Zohar*.

A Crack in the Heart

Leonard Cohen says
That there's a crack in everything.
That's how the light gets in.

Yet I wonder,
If what feels like a crack
Suddenly in my core,
A crack
Suddenly in my life,
Is how it feels
In the moment
That God has chosen
To place a *tzohar* in me,
To wound my life,
And to open my spirit,
In order to insert a gem of radiant light
Into my heart
That now shines from inside me,
From my soul to yours,
Outward into eternity.

There's a crack in everything.
That's how the light gets out.

חֹשֶׁךְ
Choshech, Darkness

THE NINTH PLAGUE on Egypt—after the locusts and before the death of the firstborn—is *choshech*, 'darkness,' also defined as 'obscurity.' The root *chet-shin-chaf* means 'to be or grow dark.'

The Torah first uses *choshech* in the description of the earth's state prior to Creation. "On the chaotic waters' face there was darkness" (Genesis 1:2). This darkness, the Talmud relates (*Chagigah* 11b), teaches us not to inquire what preceded Creation, an admonishment that the Sages themselves fail to keep (for example, *P'sachim* 54a and *N'darim* 39b).

The word is used three times in the verses describing the plague of darkness (Exodus 10:21–22). Each use is slightly different: *vihi choshech*, *v'yameish choshech*, and *vay'hi choshech afeilah*: 'darkness will appear,' 'darkness will be tangible,' and 'there was a thick darkness.' The phrases represent a progressive intensity of the darkness.

Rashi says that *vihi choshech*, 'darkness will appear,' means that the natural darkness darkened to a higher degree than the darkness of night; that is, the darkness of night became even darker and more black. Ibn Ezra says that *v'yameish choshech*, 'darkness will be tangible,' means that the Egyptians could feel the darkness with their hands. It was so thick that neither a candle nor fire could give off light. Sforno adds that *v'yameish choshech* removed the normal darkness called 'night' and replaced it with a form of darkness unable to interact with light at all. It was a totally different kind of darkness, which had density and texture. According to Rabbeinu Bachya, it is a darkness that continually deepens.

The final step in the progression, *vay'hi choshech afeilah*, employs a synonym: *afeilah* means 'darkness, gloominess, calamity,' and in this case 'supernatural darkness.' According to some, Chizkuni and Radak among them, *afeilah* is not just the absence of all light, but rather a created presence, just as light is a created entity; it is a darkness that darkens darkness.

Darkness and Light

If it is true
That there is a darkness
That consumes light,
A darkness that makes
Darker darkness
Alive,
So alive that you can touch it,
Taste it,
Smell it,
Cold and thick
As liquid emptiness,
A darkness that frightens itself...

Then it must be true
That there is a light
That consumes darkness,
A radiance that makes
Brilliant brilliance
Alive,
So alive that you can touch it,
Taste it,
Smell it,
Warm and bright
As liquid sunshine,
A light that
Blesses Creation.

בְּרָכָה
B'rachah, Blessing

BLESSINGS ABOUND in Torah. Wildlife, people, individuals, and Creation are all blessed by God. God blesses the Sabbath day (Genesis 2:3) and gifts the Israelites with the three-part Priestly Blessing (Numbers 6:23–27). The root of *b'rachah* is bet-reish-chaf, meaning 'to bless.' According to Klein, it might be connected it to a parallel Ugaritic root likely meaning 'strengthen,' suggesting that the original meaning was 'to be strong,' which developed into 'bless.'

Some scholars connect this Hebrew root to another root with the same letters, meaning 'knee, to kneel.' The symbolism is alluring: kneeling as an act of supplication. The evidence for a connection between 'bless' and 'kneel' is contested. Both Klein and Avraham Even-Shoshan, author of a classic Hebrew dictionary, list them with different roots and separate etymologies. Yet the metaphoric power of a single root for 'bless' and 'kneel' has entered our collective Jewish consciousness.

In the first three verses of Genesis 12, the word *b'rachah* appears five times. Nechama Leibowitz notes that this corresponds to the five appearances of the word *or*, 'light,' in Genesis 1:1–5. Leibowitz writes that just as God uses light in creating the physical world, God uses blessing in the creation of the Jewish people.

In a single chapter in Genesis, *b'rachah* is used three different ways: Abraham is blessed by God (24:1), Abraham's servant Eliezer blesses God (24:27, 48), and Rebekah's family blesses her on her journey (24:60). Taken together, we see that God blesses a human, humans bless another human, and a human blesses God.

Does God need our blessings? We are explicitly told that after eating and being satisfied, we are to bless God (Deuteronomy 8:10). Chizkuni, among others, says that this should be understood as either greeting or praising. Rabbeinu Bachya says that the idea of the created blessing the Creator is surprising. He says that by blessing God we add a dimension of God's holiness into the universe. Our blessings become the cause for more of God's creatures to receive divine blessing. In keeping with the Ugaritic root 'to strengthen,' our blessings strengthen God's blessings.

Blessing God

The secret
To blessing God
Hides in the absurdity
Of the very idea,
The paradox of God
Needing
Or wanting
Our blessings.

The secret
To blessing God
Is in releasing
The burden of expectations,
In surrendering hopes and dreams,
To find the love
Of the Holy One
That your heart yearns to sing.

The secret
To blessing God
Dances in the joy
Of the very idea,
The thrill of setting free
The songs of our souls,
The joy of sending
The love for our Maker
To the gates of heaven.

אָרוּר
Arur, Cursed

IN A MOMENt of high drama, the Israelites, about to enter the Promised Land, are told that upon entering the land they will be divided into two groups of six tribes. Half the tribes will ascend Mount Gerizim; the other half will ascend Mount Ebal. Standing between the mountains, the Levites will declare aloud twelve curses, and the people are to respond, "Amen" (Deuteromony 27:12–26). The Talmud (*Sotah* 32a) tells us that while only the curses are listed in this passage of Torah, the ritual that took place included both blessings and curses.

The root of *arur*—'cursed, damned, damnable'—is *alef-reish-reish*, meaning 'to curse.' The base, according to Klein, occurs only in Hebrew and in Akkadian. *Arur* is used throughout the Torah: The serpent is cursed for tempting Eve (Genesis 3:14). The ground is cursed as a result of Adam's failure (Genesis 3:17). Cain is cursed to be an earthly wanderer after murdering his brother (Genesis 4:11–12). Balaam is told by God that he will not be able curse the Israelites on Balak's behalf, as the people are blessed (Numbers 22:10–12, 20, 35, 23:20). In the strangest ritual described in Torah—the ordeal called *sotah*, testing the marital fidelity of a woman accused of adultery—the accused woman must drink a vile and life-threatening concoction called bitter and cursed water (Numbers 5:12–31).

According to *Midrash Tanchuma*, God began the account of Creation with the letter *bet* of the word *b'reishit* because *bet* is also the first letter of the word *baruch*, 'blessed.' *Alef* was not suitable, being the first letter of the word *arur*.

The ritual on the two mountains is followed by a second listing of curses and blessings (Deuteromomy 28), which is parallel but not identical to another list of curses (Leviticus 26). The curses are traditionally called *tocheichot*, 'rebukes.' It is customary, when reading the curses out loud on Shabbat, to chant them quickly in *soto voce*, a concession to the ancient superstition that speaking the curses may bring them about.

If There Must Be Curses

Every bone in my body,
Every drop of blood in my veins,
Every cell of my being,
Rejects the idea
That God uses curses
As punishments.

Curses, some say,
Are consequences
Of withholding love
From God.
True,
Maybe,
Sometimes,
But not always,
Maybe never.
Just ask Job.

But if there must be curses, then . . .
Cursed be despots, that their grip on power is severed
    from their hands.
Cursed be plague and disease, that they dissolve into
    impotence.
Cursed be cancer, that its insidiousness withers into
    fruitlessness.
Cursed be racism, that its teeth fall rotten from
    its mouth.
Cursed be sexual abuse, that its rage devours
    its own loins.
Cursed be the tools of war, that weapons of
    destruction melt away.
Cursed be violence, that hatred flees from the
    face of the earth.

מָן
Man, Manna

WHEN THE CHILDREN OF ISRAEL saw that a fine and flaky substance lay on the ground, a substance as fine as frost, they asked, "What is it?" (Exodus 16:15).

The first appearance of *man*—manna, the food that God provides the Israelites in the wilderness—is part of a two-word clause, *man hu*. The clause is typically translated in Torah commentaries as 'What is it?' *Man* has two entries in Klein: a noun 'manna,' and the pronoun 'what,' thus the translation 'What is it?' As a pronoun it is a hapax legomenon, emphasizing the special nature of this substance.

Rabbeinu Bachya says *man* is derived from *manah*, 'gift.' Rabbeinu Chananel says that the words *man hu* should be read as *mei-ayin*, 'Where does it come from?' since the Israelites did not know its origin. Rashbam says the expression should be read as 'Whose is it?'

The daily appearance of manna for nearly forty years is the longest running miracle in the *Tanach*. The Talmud (*Yoma* 76a) asks why the manna did not fall once a year, instead of coming down every day. One explanation: the daily appearance of manna would keep the people focused on daily acknowledgment of and dependence on God.

The Rabbis are fascinated with the flavor of manna. Torah says it tasted like coriander and rich cream (Numbers 11:7–8) and like wafers with honey (Exodus 16:31). Ibn Ezra says that the flavor changed with cooking, from wafers with honey to a cake baked in oil. Chizkuni says that when it was ground and baked, it tasted like sweet cake with cream.

One claim is that manna fell in a variety of forms (*Yoma* 75a). For the righteous, it fell as baked bread; for average people, it fell as unbaked cakes; for the wicked it came in an unprocessed form, requiring them to grind it in a mill. In any case, manna was the source of bread throughout the journey.

Rabbi Y'hudah HeChasid wrote in *Sefer HaChasidim* that the blessing before eating manna parallels the *HaMotzi* blessing we say before eating bread, ending with the modified phrase *hamotzi lechem min hashamayim*, 'Blessed are You, *Adonai* our God, who brings forth bread from heaven.'

Source of Bread

What is bread
Without a blessing?
It feeds the body
But not the soul.
Let sustenance lead me
To You.

What is water
Without a blessing?
It quenches the thirst
But not the yearning.
Let sustenance lead me
To You.

Let life flow with bread and water,
With milk and honey,
With bounty and plenty for all.
Let no one go hungry,
Not for food,
And not for You,
Source of life,
Not for You,
Source of all.

פֶּסֶל
Pesel, Idol

THE TORAH'S PROHIBITION against idolatry, pervasive in the text and throughout Rabbinic literature, is as blunt as possible in Deuteronomy: "Cursed be anyone who makes a sculptured or molten image, abhorred by the Eternal, a craftsman's handiwork" (27:15). As with all the curses, the people answer, "Amen."

According to several sources—*M'chilta D'Rabbi Yishmael*, *Sifra K'doshim*, and *Avot D'Rabbi Natan*—there are ten synonyms for 'idol,' although the specific words included vary. The two synonyms for 'idol' that are used in the curse—*pesel* and *maseichah*—appear on all three lists. A *pesel* is an engraved image; *maseichah* is a molten image.

The root of *pesel*, *pei-samech-lamed*, means 'to hew out, carve.' The same letters are the root of the word *pasul*, here meaning 'to disqualify, declare unfit.' Klein notes that some scholars link the two roots. *Pesel* would have originally meant 'was cut away,' from which the meaning 'was considered useless' arose, with the resulting *psolet*, 'chips, stone dust,' becoming 'worthless matter.' The hewn idol is worthless and disqualified. Other scholars see the two roots as separate word bases.

The verb form of *pesel*—'to hew, cut, chisel'—is used when God tells Moses to cut two new tablets of stone for the Ten Commandments to replace the two that Moses broke upon witnessing the *eigel maseichah*, the 'molten calf,' that is, the Golden Calf. The same action, chiseling stone, can be used to promote God's commandments or to break them.

In *Avot D'Rabbi Natan* we learn that there are ten names that refer to God and ten words for idolatry. Malbim says that this symmetry teaches that there is equal power to the forces of good and evil. According to Rabbi Reuven Chaim Klein, this balance allows for the freewill choice between the two.

The Idol Maker

The idol maker is crafty,
Beckoning us to worship
At the feet of human invention.

This god is for love. This god is for wealth.
This god is for beauty. This god is for sweet dreams.

The idol maker lives next door,
Inviting us in with the smell of fresh bread
And intoxication,
To lull us to sleep
And forget our God.

"Come carve with me,"
The idol maker says,
"We will make our gods together."

Beware,
For the idol maker,
Who yearns for rock and silver,
Will use your soul as chiseling stone,
To form lifeless objects,
To divide you from yourself,
To keep you from reaching
The Holy One,
The *Shechinah*,
The *Ein Sof*,
The Divine One,
Godself,
Your Creator
And Salvation.

רְפָא
R'fa, Heal

WITH FIVE SIMPLE WORDS, Moses entreats God to heal his sister Miriam's snowy scales: "O God, pray heal her!" (Numbers 12:13). The plea is made in the imperative form, yet Miriam must be punished, and this demand-as-prayer for immediate healing is rejected.

The root of *r'fa*, the verb 'to heal, cure,' is *reish-pei-alef*. It is a contranym, also meaning 'to weaken.' David Curwin offers, "In general in Biblical Hebrew, when that root ends with the letter *alef* it means 'to heal,' and when it ends with the letter *hey*, it means 'to weaken,' but there are exceptions. It's unclear whether the two meanings are etymologically related. One possibility is that 'to weaken' refers to the illness, not the individual who is sick."

Among the laws regulating civil behavior, the Torah requires that damages be paid to one who is injured at the hand of another (Exodus 21:19). The language includes a puzzling compound use of two forms of the word: *v'rapo y'rapei*. Typically, this doubled structure indicates intensity, meaning 'he shall surely heal.' This is perplexing because the assailant cannot be trusted or even called upon to heal the victim. The rabbis—including Ibn Ezra and Or HaChayim—interpret it to mean that the assailant must pay civil damages.

From the doubled form, Ibn Ezra understands that humans are granted God's permission to heal wounds and blows on the body. He notes that *y'rapei* is in the intensifying *pi-eil* (causative, emphatic) verb form, which implies an expenditure of effort that God would not need in order to heal, but a human would. Ibn Ezra concludes that human assistance for healing cuts and bruises is permissible. The Talmud and *Tosafot* go further in permitting medical intervention. The *Tosafot* on *Bava Kama* 85a concludes that permission is granted to a doctor to heal; medical intervention is not considered to be counter to God's will.

The Chief Physician

While Moses was
Appointing judges
And creating courts,
While Aaron
Was tending the altar
And leading priests,
Miriam was training doctors
And creating clinics
To tend the wounds
And the hearts
Of the people.

Only a healer
Could find hidden water
In the desert wilderness.

Only a healer
Could dance with passion
In the narrow space
Between life and death.

For the healer
Shall surely heal,
And the prophetess
Shall surely bring blessings.

אָמֵן
Amen, Truly

IN THE TALMUD (*Shabbat* 119b), Reish Lakish says that the gates of Eden open for those who say *amen* with all their strength. Rabbi Y'hoshua ben Levi adds that responding to prayers with *amen* has the power to annul evil decrees. Speaking in the name of Rabbi Yochanan, Rabbi Chiya bar Abba says that when one answers a prayer with *amen*, even those people with traces of idolatry in their hearts are forgiven.

This simple word—ubiquitous in our prayers and blessings, as well as in vernacular speech—has profound power. *Amen* means 'verily, truly, so be it, to accept something as true.' The root, *alef-mem-nun*, is also the root of three other powerful words: *emunah*, 'faith'; *ne-eman*, 'faithful'; and *maamin*, 'to believe.' The root can be found in a variety of Semitic languages, including Ethiopian, Old South Arabic, and Syrian. The fundamental idea of them all: stability, steadfastness, and reliability.

On the same page of Talmud, Rabbi Chanina says that the letters *alef-mem-nun* are an acronym for *El Melech ne-eman*, 'God, faithful Sovereign.' The phrase *El Melech ne-eman* is traditionally said before a private recitation of the *Sh'ma*. When we say *amen*, we affirm both the prayer and our faith in the Almighty.

The Sages of the Talmud list three ineffective ways to say *amen* (*B'rachot* 47a): the hurried or abbreviated *amen* is when the first syllable is not properly enunciated; the truncated *amen* is when the second syllable is not properly enunciated; and the orphaned *amen* occurs when the person saying it is unaware of the blessing to which they are responding. In other words, as much as any prayer, saying *amen* requires attention and intention.

Rashi says that *amen* implies the acceptance of an oath that has been recited by another person on one's behalf. In *D'varim Rabbah* 7:1, Rabbi Y'hudah bar Shimon says that *amen* has three elements: oath, acceptance, and faithfulness.

Amen

When you have
No words to pray,
Say Amen
To your own heart.

When you have
No words to pray,
Say Amen
To God's Creation.

When you have
No words to pray,
Say Amen
To bless those you love.

God, faithful Sovereign.
Amen

Love

❧

וְעַתָּה יִשְׂרָאֵל מָה יהוה אֱלֹהֶיךָ שֹׁאֵל מֵעִמָּךְ
כִּי אִם־לְיִרְאָה אֶת יהוה אֱלֹהֶיךָ לָלֶכֶת
בְּכָל־דְּרָכָיו וּלְאַהֲבָה אֹתוֹ וְלַעֲבֹד אֶת יהוה אֱלֹהֶיךָ
בְּכָל־לְבָבְךָ וּבְכָל־נַפְשֶׁךָ.

And now, O Israel, what does the Eternal your God demand of you?
Only this: to revere the Eternal your God, to walk only in divine paths,
and to love and serve the Eternal your God
with all your heart and with all your soul.
—Deuteronomy 10:12

THE WORDS *AHAVAH* (love) and *l'vavcha* (your heart) appear together
three times in Deuteronomy. Each time we are commanded to love
God fully, twice with all our hearts and souls (10:12, 30:6). The third
time, in perhaps the most famous verse, we are commanded to love
God with all our heart, soul, and might (6:5). Our exploration of love
begins with two words about being fully present, *hineini* (here I am)
and *l'vavcha*. The exploration continues with four ways we can put
love into action: *s'lichah* (forgiveness), *tzedek* (justice), *rachum* (merciful), and *zachor* (remember). This section, and the book, closes with
the word *ot* (sign) to help us *zachor*—remember—that signs of God's
love are all around us.

Recitations of the *Sh'ma* are preceded with prayers reminding us of
God's love: in the morning *Ahavah Rabbah* and in the evening *Ahavat
Olam*. Before we declare our fealty to the One God, we remember the
Divine's love for us. The Talmud (*B'rachot* 33b) relates that everything
is in the hand of heaven except for *yirat shamayim*, 'fear of heaven'
or 'reverence for heaven.' Perhaps we are commanded to love God
because that is the essence of free will: the choice to love God. In
other words, it is up to us to love God, to walk in divine paths, and to
serve God completely and without hesitation.

הִנֵּנִי
Hineini, Here I Am

Just before asking Abraham to sacrifice his son on an altar, God calls out to the patriarch by name. "Abraham!" God says. Abraham answers: *Hineini*, "Here I am" (Genesis 22:1). In our spiritual consciousness, this one-word response has become the quintessential reply to a call from God, as the complete acknowledgment of God's authority and our absolute willingness to do what is asked of us. This is not so easy, when it might mean sacrificing one's child.

Hineini is the combination *hinei*, with a first-person suffix. *Hinei* is an interjection, a word expressing a spontaneous feeling or reaction, meaning 'lo, behold, yes, here.' Commonly translated as 'Here I am,' *The Living Torah* translates it simply as 'yes,' noting in a footnote that *hineini* is an idiomatic answer to a summons.

Hineini marks many major moments in the lives of the Patriarchs, as well as the start of the Exodus from Egypt. The word appears three times in the Binding of Isaac, first when God calls to Abraham, then when Isaac calls out to his father (Genesis 22:7), and finally when the angel stops the sacrifice (22:11). When Jacob tricks his blind father Isaac into giving him and not Esau a blessing, Jacob calls out, "*Avi*"—'my father'—and Isaac responds, "*Hineini*" (27:18). When Jacob summons his favorite son Joseph to send him off to look after his brothers, Joseph answers, "*Hineini*" (37:13). In a dream, after Jacob has set out to meet his long-lost son Joseph, God calls out and Jacob responds, "*Hineini*" (46:2). When God calls to Moses from the Burning Bush, Moses answers, "*Hineini*" (Exodus 3:4).

Reb Zalman Schachter-Shalomi wrote that the *g'matria* of the word *hineini* is 115, the same as *anachnu* (we), *aliyah* (ascent), and *ha-am* (the people). The implication: by declaring *hineini*, we become part of the larger *k'neset Yisrael*—the whole house of Israel—transcending ourselves and joining the fate of the Jewish people. He wrote, "By being counted in *hineini*, we become part of the larger 'we,' *anachnu*; we experience an ascent, an *aliyah* of awareness that frees us from the narrowness of I-ness; and thus we become part of *ha-am*, the people."

Hineini, Waiting

The first *hineini*
Was silent.
It was not a declaration.
Not an announcement.
Not "look at me, I'm ready."
Not a summons to God.
The first *hineini* was silent.
It happened before the word was spoken.

Hineini is opening heart.
Hineini is clearing mind.
Hineini is simple readiness.
Wait. Breathe. Surrender.

Hineini is the act of preparing
For God to call your name.
Wait. Breathe. Surrender.

And when you hear the call, declare:
"Amen to my prayer."
And "Hallelujah, God has called my name."
This moment is unlike any other,
For God has summoned me.
Hineini.

Yes, God, here I am.
I've been waiting.
I've been hoping.
I've been dreaming.

Before you say *hineini* with your lips,
Say it with your life.

לְבָבְךָ
L'vavcha, Your Heart

THIS VERSE may be one of the most familiar pieces of Torah to Jews throughout the world: "You shall love the Eternal your God with all your heart, with all your soul, and with all your might" (Deuteronomy 6:5). It might be second in familiarity only to the line that precedes it: "Hear, O Israel! *Adonai* is our God, *Adonai* is One" (6:4).

L'vavcha is composed of the root *lamed-bet-bet* and the pronominal suffix *-cha*, meaning 'your.' The root is a related form of the two-letter stem *lamed-bet*: *lev*, which means 'heart, mind, will.' In biblical times the essential meaning of 'heart' differed from how we understand the metaphor of the heart today. Unlike our view that the heart is the seat of emotion, in Biblical Hebrew *lev* refers to the seat of intellectual thoughts and ideas.

The Rabbis note that *l'vavcha* could have been spelled without the second *bet*. In *Mishnah B'rachot* 9:5, they explain that the double *bet* represents both the *yetzer hatov* and the *yetzer hara* (the good inclination and the evil inclination), which are part of each human. As a result, the verse "with all your heart" means to love God with both aspects of the human character: one's inclination to good and one's inclination to evil. Rabbi Shoshana Meira Friedman takes this idea a step further, saying that we are complex beings, with parts that are "protective, joyful, traumatized, optimistic, shy, empowered," and more. We can love God with all the complex pieces of our humanity.

Loving God is a dominant theme in Deuteronomy. The forms *l'vavcha* and *l'vavecha* are used only twenty times in Torah, with nineteen of them in Deuteronomy. The midrash (*Sifrei D'varim* 32) holds that love of God is best expressed when we conduct ourselves in a way that makes God beloved by others.

The Language of Your Soul

The language of your soul,
That fountain of blessings inside you,
Pouring forth in a river of delight
From you to God
And God to you,
Sustaining life and Creation itself,
Singing goodness,
And beauty,
And truth,
Can only be summoned
From the secret chambers
Of your heart.

Let the language of your soul
Sing all around you,
Drawing others into the music,
Drawing others into the song,
The rhythm of the universe,
Which is, was, and always will be
Love.

סְלִיחָה
S'lichah, Forgiveness

As a noun, the word s'lichah, 'forgiveness,' appears only three times in Tanach, none of them in the Torah, where it appears only as a verb, in a variety of forms. The first use in Torah comes after the incident of the Golden Calf, when Moses prays for God to forgive the people (Exodus 34:9). God tells Moses that the Divine Presence will withdraw from the people as a result of this grievous sin, and instead an angel will lead them forward. Bowing to the ground, Moses makes an impassioned plea for forgiveness, asking God to remain in the midst of the people.

According to Klein, the root is samech-lamed-chet, 'to forgive, pardon,' deriving from the Akkadian salāḫu, meaning 'to sprinkle.' It is related to the Aramaic-Syriac word z'lach (zayin-lamed-chet), meaning 'he poured out, sprinkled.' Klein notes that z'lach is related to another root, zayin-lamed-gimel, meaning 'to drip, flow,' which may be derived from the Ethiopian zalḥa, 'he poured forth tears.' Thus, the word 'forgive' flows from water.

In many faiths, immersion in water is an ancient rite of purification. In Judaism, even today, immersion in the mikveh, the ritual bath, is a commonly practiced renewal and purification ritual. Torah and Tanach often speak of being cleansed from sin. It is not a stretch to see how the lexicon for "forgiveness" might derive from words for flowing water. Forgiveness has a cleansing power.

Before Moses asks for forgiveness, God reveals the thirteen attributes of divine mercy, declaring that God forgives inequity, transgression, and sin (Exodus 34:7). Here God uses a different word to describe divine 'forgiveness'—nakei, which means 'clean.' God's eternal promise to cleanse away sin is also connected to water.

To Be Free

Let the well of forgiveness
Wash me clean.
How I wish
To be free
Of evil thoughts and callous deeds.
How I wish
To be worthy in Your sight.
To receive a heart refreshed,
And a soul that shines.
To be free
Of iniquity, transgression, and sin,
To emerge from the waters of Your mercy,
Into the light of Your love.

צֶדֶק
Tzedek, Justice

THE JEWISH IMPERATIVE to pursue justice is summarized in three words: *Tzedek tzedek tirdof*, "Justice, justice shall you pursue" (Deuteronomy 16:20). The repetition is both poetic and powerful. As is typical, it's just this repetition that has the creative minds of the Rabbis spinning.

Tzedek, meaning 'justice, righteousness,' is also the meaning of its root, *tzadi-dalet-kof*. According to Klein, the root is related to a variety of words, including the Ugaritic *ṣdq*, 'reliability, virtue'; the Arabic *ṣadaqa*, 'he spoke the truth'; and the Ethiopian *ṣadaqa*, 'he was just, he was righteous.'

Rashi says that the repetition of *tzedek tzedek* means that one should seek a reliable court. Ibn Ezra says it means that we must pursue justice whether one wins or loses in court. It also indicates that pursuing justice is a lifetime endeavor. Ramban, quoting a midrash, says that the first reference to *tzedek* refers to pursing justice in this world. The second *tzedek*—referring to the messianic days—is meant to frighten the righteous that they may not merit a place in the world-to-come. Sforno writes that the repetition is an instruction to Moses to seek judges already known for their sense of fair play and righteousness. The Talmud (*Sanhedrin* 32b) says that this is an instruction to follow the best, most prestigious court of the generation.

In *Parashat K'doshim*, the Israelites are commanded to use honest weights and measures. Employing the word *tzedek*, the commandment might be more literally translated as 'righteous' weights and measures (Leviticus 19:36).

In Biblical Hebrew, *tzedek* and *tzedakah* are essentially synonyms. They are nouns, the former masculine and the latter feminine, both meaning 'justice' and 'righteousness.' According to David Curwin, *tzedek* more often refers to the concept or value of justice, but *tzedakah* more frequently refers to performing acts of justice in the world. Only in postbiblical Hebrew has the word *tzedakah* taken on the meaning of 'charity given to the poor.'

Honest Weights and Measures

God commands us
To use honest weights and measures.
Not to cheat.
Not to deceive.
Not to swindle.
To be righteous in commerce.

What about
An honest eye,
An honest hand,
An honest heart?
Do not cheat another with a critical eye.
Do not deceive another with a dishonest hand.
Do not swindle another with a judgmental heart.

Let my acts of kindness and mercy,
Tenderness and grace,
Charity and forgiveness,
Pile up as a mountain of stones,
On the scale of righteousness
And on the scale of love.

רַחוּם
Rachum, Merciful

THE THIRTEEN ATTRIBUTES of divine mercy are a central refrain in
the Yom Kippur liturgy. From Exodus 34:6–7 we repeat several times:
"Adonai, Adonai—God, compassionate, gracious, endlessly patient,
loving, and true; showing mercy to the thousandth generation, for-
giving evil, defiance, and wrongdoing; granting pardon" (*Mishkan
HaNefesh*). For all its centrality in our liturgy and in our understanding of
God's true nature, the word for merciful—*rachum*—is rare in the Torah.

The root is *reish-chet-mem*, the same as the word for 'womb,' *rechem*.
Rabbi Minna Bromberg teaches that a womb can be thought of as the
ideal of mercy: literally giving of oneself by creating and holding protected space for someone else to form, take shape, and grow.

As an adjective, *rachum* appears only twice in the Torah. The first
occurrence as an adjective is at a pivotal moment: the recitation of the
thirteen attributes—God's own description of Godself—proclaimed
to Moses as God's countenance passes near to him. That promise of
divine mercy is echoed in the second use of *rachum* as an adjective, when
Moses reiterates God's promise of mercy (Deuteronomy 4:31).

The verb *racheim* appears only four times. Again, the first use is pivotal. It comes in the chapter before the thirteen attributes, when God
promises to reveal God's goodness to Moses. We learn that God's mercy
is mysterious when the Almighty says, "I will be gracious to whom I will
be gracious, and will show mercy on whom I will show mercy" (Exodus
33:19, Soncino).

As the noun, *rachamim*, defined by Klein as 'intense compassion,' it
appears only four times in the Torah. In its first use, Jacob prays for the
safe return of his sons: Simeon, who is being held hostage by Joseph,
and Benjamin, who must travel with his older brothers to redeem Simeon and buy grain (Genesis 43:14).

Forms of the word appear throughout our liturgy, reinforcing our
connection with the divine attribute of mercy. It appears nine times
in the weekday morning *T'filah* alone and four more in the rest of the
morning service, more than its total use in all of Torah.

Where Is Mercy?

Adonai, Adonai—
God compassionate, gracious, and kind,
Showing mercy to the thousandth generation,
Where will we find Your mercy
In a world of war and plague,
Of pain and pandemic,
Of random killing and premeditated violence?
Where will we find
Your mercy,
When Your countenance
Stays hidden?

Mercy is now
In our hands,
In our deepest prayers,
And we will do
Your work of grace and kindness,
Providing healing
To a struggling world.
We are Your well of mercy,
And Your fountain of compassion.

זָכוֹר
Zachor, Remember

GOD REMEMBERS, and God wants us to remember. The word *zachor*—from the root *zayin-chaf-reish*—means 'to remember' and is used in Torah to describe acts of God and actions of people. The first use occurs when God remembers Noah in the ark (Genesis 8:1). At various moments, God remembers Abraham (Genesis 19:29), Rachel (Genesis 30:22), and the Israelites in Egyptian captivity (Exodus 2:24). God remembers the covenant with our ancestors (Leviticus 26:42, 45), and Moses asks God to remember that covenant (Exodus 32:13). Moments of memory are often pivotal—for example, when the chief cupbearer remembers that Joseph can interpret dreams (Genesis 41:9).

Some scholars hold that the root originally meant 'to pierce.' This creates a link with the other meaning for the root, 'male,' alluding to the function of the male member in procreation. David Curwin says that *zachor* moved from 'to pierce' to 'to fix in one's mind' to 'remember.'

God commands the people to remember six specific moments in history, with five found in Deuteronomy: remember the Exodus from Egypt (Deuteronomy 16:3), Revelation at Sinai (4:9–10), Amalek's attack on Israel (25:17–19), the Golden Calf and the rebellion in the desert (9:7), and Miriam's negative speech and her punishment (24:9).

The instruction to remember the violence of Amalek attacking the Israelites from behind is strangely formulated. We are told to "remember what Amalek did to you on your journey" (Deuteronomy 25:17), adding that "you shall blot out the memory of Amalek from under heaven. Do not forget!" (25:19). In other words, remember to forget.

The sixth remembrance is to "Remember the Sabbath day and keep it holy" (Exodus 20:8). This has an alternative formulation: "Observe the Sabbath day and keep it holy" (Deuteronomy 5:12). The shift from *zachor* to *shamor*—'to guard, to observe'—has led to an interpretation that *zachor Shabbat* means to remember the very first occurrence of the Sabbath to keep it holy, the one day of God's initial rest from the work of Creation. *Shamor Shabbat* is to guard and observe the sanctity of each new Shabbat that occurs weekly.

Remember, Forget

Remember the Sabbath day
To keep it holy,
The only one that ever occurred,
The day God rested.
And remember this Sabbath day
To keep it holy,
The one, the only one,
That will arrive this week.

Remember to forget
The name of the wickedness
That stalks the weak
And the wounded
From behind,
Ready to claim
Casualties of the body, mind, and spirit.
Blot out the evil.
Remember to forget.

Memory,
Beyond the bonds of time,
Stretches from before Creation
To the end of eternity,
Like a bird who carries
All we know,
And all we have forgotten,
From generation to generation.

We are
What we remember
And what we choose
To forget.

אוֹת
Ot, Sign

IN THE FIRST seventeen chapters of Genesis, the word *ot*—'sign, signal, symbol, token'—is used alternatively to describe the sun and the moon as signs to mark days, years, and God's appointed seasons (1:14); the mark placed upon Cain to protect him from vengeance (4:15); the rainbow as a symbol of the covenant that God will never again destroy the world by water (9:12–13, 17); and circumcision as a sign of the covenant between Abraham and God (17:11).

Moses is given signs to convince the people that he spoke with God: his rod turning into a snake, his hand becoming leprous and then being healed, and pouring water from the Nile, which then turns into blood (Exodus 4:1–8).

Throughout the Exodus and the wandering of the Israelites, God performs "signs and wonders," *otot umoftim* (e.g., Deuteronomy 6:22), here used in the plural. Although a secondary definition of *ot* is 'miracle,' Rabbi Jonathan Sacks makes a strong distinction between signs, *otot*, and wonders, *moftim*, which might be thought of as special displays of God's power. An *ot*, a sign, has a purpose: to teach a lesson, to show something critical to the Israelites and the world. Sacks calls *otot* coded messages from God.

According to the Ramban, that's a two-way street. Although apparently there are no more signs coming *from* God—in the sense of miraculous events that have hidden messages—every commandment that is fulfilled is a sign *to* God, a message that we, the descendants of the Israelites, still remember the *otot umoftim* performed on our behalf.

Celebrating Shabbat and the Festivals brings that holiness back into our lives and is a sign of our devotion to God's appointed times and season. Wearing *t'fillin* is the practice understood from God's instruction to bind God's word as a sign upon our hands and as symbols between our eyes, which radiate back to God our love for the Divine (Deuteronomy 11:18).

Ours Now

There's no use
Waiting for a pillar of cloud
To descend from the sky,
Or a pillar of fire
To lead the way.

Some ask:
Where are the signs and wonders
In our day?
Where has God's voice
Been hidden away?

The signs and wonders
Are still with us,
In our hearts and minds.
In our lives.
They are ours now,
To remember,
To reenact,
To send back to heaven,
As a sign from us.

Bibliographic Essay

THESE WORDS: *Poetic Midrash on the Language of Torah* is informed by significant research. Because it is not intended as a scholarly endeavor, however, I've opted not to include a full, formal bibliography. For readers who are interested, the resources I relied upon most heavily are presented below. This list is not intended to be comprehensive; rather, it is meant to give readers a window into the work and a doorway into conducting their own explorations.

Two websites played a central role in this research, Alhatorah.org and Sefaria.org. Every day of research, both of these sites were open in multiple windows on my desktop simultaneously.

Research on each word began with Alhatorah's Concordance and Dictionary, which includes modified versions of J. Strong, *The Exhaustive Concordance of the Bible* (1890); F. Brown, S. R. Driver, and C. A. Briggs, *A Hebrew and English Lexicon of the Old Testament* (1906); and the work of D. Troidl from openscriptures.org. Along with the core concordance and dictionary, I relied regularly on two key features: the charting feature was particularly useful in gaining an overview of where the word appears in *Tanach*, while the advanced search function allowed me to easily search the concordance for passages containing multiple words of interest.

Much of the heavy lifting took place on Sefaria. It was my go-to location for Torah commentary and access to English-language translations of midrash, Talmud, and other *sifrei kodesh*, as well an etymological dictionary. Sefaria provided access to a wide variety of resources, including E. Klein, *A Comprehensive Etymological Dictionary of the Hebrew Language, for Readers of English* (1987); Marcus Jastrow, *A Dictionary of the Targumim, the Talmud Bavli and Yerushalmi, and the Midrashic Literature* (1903); and the *William Davidson digital edition of the Koren Noé Talmud, with commentary by Rabbi Adin Even-Israel Steinsaltz*. Sefaria also provided *Tanach* and Talmud commentary from the *Rishonim* (commentators who lived in the eleventh through fifteenth centuries) and *Acharonim* (commentators who lived in the sixteenth through nineteenth centuries), as well as many modern commentaries. The specific source citations for each commentator can be found on Sefaria.

Torah Commentaries

Six *Chumashim* served as core to checking translations of individual words and passages, as well as providing sources of commentary:

Cohn Eskanazi, Tamara, and Andrea L. Weiss, eds. *The Torah: A Women's Commentary*. New York: CCAR Press and Women of Reform Judaism, 2008.

Hertz, Joseph Herman, ed. *The Pentateuch and Haftorahs*. London: Soncino Press, 1981.

JPS Hebrew-English Tanakh. Philadelphia: Jewish Publication Society, 1999.

Kaplan, Aryeh. *The Living Torah*. Brooklyn: Moznaim, 1981.

Plaut, W. Gunther, ed. *The Torah: A Modern Commentary*. Rev. ed. New York: CCAR Press, 2005 (source of the Hebrew verses).

Scherman, Nosson, and Meir Zlotowitz, eds. *The Chumash: The Stone Edition*. ArtScroll Series. Brooklyn: Mesorah, 1993.

Other Resources

When the research or my creativity hit a wall, I employed a variety of strategies. One was to check an assortment of Hebrew-language scholars to see if they happened to comment on my target word, some in books, some online. Sometimes I did a general web search on a word or idea. Sometimes I conducted targeted searches of the writings of particular rabbis, scholars, or educators. Occasionally these searches yielded quotes that I incorporated into the text. Here's a list of my most frequently checked resources:

Benstein, Jeremy, *The Hebrew Corner*. 929.org.il.

Blech, Benjamin. *The Secrets of Hebrew Words*. Northvale, NJ: Jason Aronson, 1991.

Curwin, David. *Balashon: Hebrew Language Detective*. Balashon.com.

Jonathan Sacks: The Rabbi Sacks Legacy Trust. Rabbisacks.org.

Klein, Reuven Chaim. *What's in a Word?* Ohr Somayach. Ohr.edu/this_week/whats_in_a_word/.

Kushner, Lawrence. *The Book of Words: Talking Spiritual Life, Living Spiritual Talk*. Woodstock, VT: Jewish Lights, 1993.

Lowin, Joseph. *Hebrew Talk: 101 Hebrew Roots and the Stories They Tell*. Oakland, CA: EKS, 2004.

Mechon Mamre. Mechon-mamre.org.

My Jewish Learning. Myjewishlearning.com.

RavBlog. Central Conference of American Rabbis. Ravblog.ccarnet. org.

ReformJudaism.org.

As much as possible, I traced references back to a primary source. Similarly, I traced any assertion about a word found on a blog or in a book to a primary source. Facebook played a role in this effort. When I came across a reference that I couldn't find in a primary source or needed direction finding a particular resource, I posted questions on my Facebook page. Often, those postings would yield the needed reference, which I also checked.

Alphabetical Index—Hebrew

About the Author

ALDEN SOLOVY spreads joy and excitement for prayer. An American Israeli liturgist, poet, author, and educator, he has written nearly one thousand pieces of new liturgy, offering a fresh, new Jewish voice that often challenges the boundaries between prayer, poetry, meditation, personal growth, and storytelling. His writing was transformed by multiple tragedies, marked in 2009 by the sudden death of his wife from catastrophic brain injury. The liturgist-in-residence for the Pardes Institute of Jewish Studies in Jerusalem, his teaching spans from Hebrew Union College–Jewish Institute of Religion and the Conservative Yeshiva in Jerusalem to synagogues throughout North America, as well as Leo Baeck College in London and Limmud conferences in the United States, Canada, and the United Kingdom. He is the author of five books, three from CCAR Press: *This Precious Life: Encountering the Divine with Poetry and Prayer, This Joyous Soul: A New Voice for Ancient Yearnings,* and *This Grateful Heart: Psalms and Prayers for a New Day.* Alden's work is anthologized in more than twenty volumes from Jewish, Christian, and Catholic publishers, including the following CCAR Press editions: *Mishkan R'fuah: Where Healing Resides* (2012), *L'chol Z'man v'Eit: For Sacred Moments* (2015), *Mishkan HaNefesh: Machzor for the Days of Awe* (2015), *Gates of Shabbat,* revised edition (2016), *Mishkan Aveilut: Where Grief Resides* (2019), and *Mishkan Ga'avah: Where Pride Dwells* (2020). Alden also writes for Ritualwell, *RavBlog,* ReformJudaism.org, and the Times of Israel. He is a three-time winner of the Peter Lisagor Award for Exemplary Journalism. In 2012, Alden made *aliyah* to Jerusalem. He is the founder of ManKind Project Israel. Find his latest work at www.ToBendLight.com.